THE RISE OF THE HITMAN

THE RISE OF THE HITMAN

THE **ROHIT SHARMA** STORY

R. KAUSHIK

Published by
Rupa Publications India Pvt. Ltd 2025
7/16, Ansari Road, Daryaganj
New Delhi 110002

Sales centres:
Bengaluru Chennai Hyderabad
Jaipur Kathmandu Kolkata
Mumbai Prayagraj

Copyright © R. Kaushik 2025
Photographs courtesy: Surjeet Yadav

The views and opinions expressed in this book are the author's own and the facts are as reported by them which have been verified to the extent possible, and the publishers are not in any way liable for the same.

All rights reserved.
No part of this publication may be reproduced, transmitted, or stored in a retrieval system, in any form or by any means, electronic, mechanical, photocopying, recording or otherwise, without the prior permission of the publisher.

P-ISBN: 978-93-6156-535-9
E-ISBN: 978-93-6156-924-1

First impression 2025

10 9 8 7 6 5 4 3 2 1

The moral right of the author has been asserted.

Printed in India

This book is sold subject to the condition that it shall not, by way of trade or otherwise, be lent, resold, hired out, or otherwise circulated, without the publisher's prior consent, in any form of binding or cover other than that in which it is published.

For

My Father
The greatest role model

My late Mother
My eternal guiding light

The late M.L. Jaisimha
My first and foremost cricketing mentor
&
My Muse
Brighter than the sun

Contents

Foreword by Ritika Sajdeh	ix
Introduction: The Making of a Legend	xi
Prologue: Winning the World Cup	xvii
1. Humble Beginnings	1
2. The Early Promise	9
3. A Steady Climb, and Huge Setbacks	24
4. The Birth of the White-ball Opener	36
5. White-ball Legend	47
6. The IPL Kingpin	57
7. The World Cup Behemoth	71
8. Opening Gambit	86
9. Acing the English Test	98
10. The Leadership Masterstroke	113

11. Untold Agony, Unmatched Ecstasy	128
12. A Match Made in Cricketing Heaven	143
13. The Man behind the 'Hitman'	158
14. A Lasting Legacy	172
Epilogue	183
Acknowledgements	193
Index	195

Foreword
The Ro I know and love

What can I say about this man? Words truly fail me. I met Ro in 2008 and as soon as I got to know him, I knew he would be in my life forever. Maybe not as my husband (that was a happy surprise!) but because I recognized how special he was as a human being, and I wanted that goodness in my life. He's just so unapologetically himself and that is incredibly refreshing. What you see is what you get. And people like that are hard to find. He has a heart of gold and will go that extra mile for anyone he cares about. To know Ro is to love him. Whoever's eyes you look at him through, you will see the same Ro, that's how genuine he is.

I have watched Ro strive, toil, rise up, fall down, being criticized and then raised to a level he never imagined he'd reach. But through it all, he has remained the same. The boy I met in 2008 is still the same man he is today, just a little wiser and a lot stronger mentally.

I have watched every innings Ro has played since the day I met him, be it for Mumbai in the Ranji Trophy or for India, and, just like the rest of the country, I truly love his game! It brings us joy to watch him do what he does, and his kids and I are and always will be proud of the player and the man he is. He is the most present father who takes true joy in doing small and big things with his children.

I am very proud of the man he is on the field and everything he has achieved, but what I am most proud of is his heart and everything it beats for; his game, his players, his family, his friends, the environment, animals and so much more.

I could go on and on but I'm not the one writing the book on Ro. I'll leave that to Kaushik.

Ritika Sajdeh

Introduction
The Making of a Legend

Greatness in sports isn't measured by success alone, though that's a pretty good yardstick. In cricket, success is judged by runs and wickets; titles and trophies as well, if one is the skipper. But one's impact is also evident in how lives are touched and shaped, how careers are encouraged and nurtured, how one carries himself and what their legacy ends up being. Rohit Sharma might not agree that he already falls in the category of the *greats*, but his sentiment isn't shared by millions of others.

It might be premature to start talking about Rohit and his legacy—despite having retired from Twenty20 Internationals, he is still very much an active player—but there's no denying the impact he has had on both Indian and world cricket in an international career that is now in its eighteenth year. Rohit is no longer a legend-in-the-making. Whether he likes it or not, he is already a legend—a status cemented after he led India to the T20 World Cup crown in Bridgetown.

Rohit's journey from Borivali—where he stayed with his uncle and aunt—to the most iconic cricket grounds in the world, which he graced with his obvious silken stroke-play, unacknowledged inner steel, and uncommonly sharp tactical awareness, isn't accidental. He wasn't earmarked for great things right off the bat—he was considered too laidback and casual, labels that are thrown around without care or consideration in India—but through sheer hard work and an unflagging determination that belies his charming, laugh-a-minute exterior, he has worked his way into the consciousness and affection of the cricket world, earning oodles of respect along the way.

At various stages of his career, it appeared as if time might pass Rohit by. He played for India Under-19 at the 2006 World Cup in Sri Lanka under Ravikant Shukla and broke into the senior side a year and a half later. Few knew at the time—including the two protagonists—that his inclusion in the Rahul Dravid-led One-Day International squad that travelled to Ireland and England would mushroom into an extraordinary management group a decade and a half later, with the former captain returning as the head coach, and the promising lad brimming with potential graduating into the skipper of the national side and a veritable leader of men.

Rohit's early days at the highest level were steady rather than spectacular—occasional glimpses of brilliance blunted by extended spells of inconsistency that infuriated the pundits who rightly believed that he had plenty more to offer. Cricket in general is less charitable towards batters who are dismissed playing shots rather than in defence. India is particularly impatient in this regard, although there is no difference in the final outcome—whether in attack or in defence, out is out. Simple, right?

Introduction: The Making of a Legend

Rohit rode the punches in the only manner he knew, with resilience but not resignation. To be left out of the 50-over World Cup side of 2011 hurt as much as missing out on a Test debut some 14 months prior, when he injured his ankle during a practice session on the morning of his first scheduled appearance. Instead of donning the Test cap for the first time in February 2010, he had to wait over three and a half years, till November 2013, in a series against West Indies that will be remembered for being Sachin Tendulkar's last international outing. Rohit's 177 and 111 not out in his first two innings, in his Kolkata debut and in Tendulkar's final hurrah in Mumbai, respectively, weren't mere footnotes. But if they didn't receive their immediate due, it was because of the halo surrounding the retiring legend.

Some considered Rohit's thunderous initiation into Test cricket as the passing of the baton from one Mumbaikar to another—from the established genius to a free-flowing batter who had the potential to carve his own unique identity. Things didn't exactly pan out that way; Rohit's Test career was somewhat unfulfilling for the first six years, until a masterstroke by Virat Kohli and Ravi Shastri transformed him from a middling middle-order batter to an exceptional opener and, eventually, into the country's all-format captain.

Much as Mahendra Singh Dhoni (and coach Duncan Fletcher) had done in early 2013 for the white-ball counterparts, Kohli and Shastri thrust Rohit into the unfamiliar role of a red-ball opener in October 2019. Rohit didn't need much convincing; he had already been opening in international cricket for six and a half years—if only in the two limited-overs versions—and sensed that this was an opportunity for him to fulfil the Test promise he and numerous others were convinced nestled in him. Like in his debut, he was magical in his first match as a Test opener in Visakhapatnam, celebrating his promotion with twin centuries against South Africa—unleashing another double-century for good measure later in the same series—and embarking on a journey that set him up as a reliable, all-weather long-format opening batter capable of batting in multiple gears, depending on the situation.

2019 would end up being a watershed year in Rohit's cricketing life in many ways. At the 50-over World Cup in England in the summer, he smashed five centuries—an unprecedented feat in the tournament's history—but the eventual defeat to New Zealand in the semifinal left him feeling hollow. Presented with the golden opportunity to rejuvenate his flailing Test career a few months later, he justified the faith reposed in him by his captain and head coach.

There has been no looking back since.

By then, Rohit had already led India's limited-overs side on an interim basis—stepping into the hot seat whenever Kohli was unavailable—but Test captaincy would have been the farthest from his mind when he took strike against the Proteas in Vizag. Less than two and a half years later, he had succeeded Kohli as the all-format leader, a tag that sat lightly on him. Rohit had already showcased his leadership skills by turning Mumbai Indians' fortunes around after taking over mid-season from Ricky Ponting in 2013. That was the first of five titles MI won under Rohit, whose man-management skills are second to none and whose unflappable temperament allowed him to keep his wits around him even in the tensest of situations.

In his pre-teens, Rohit was primarily viewed as an off-spinner. He is a very good one too, with an IPL hat-trick to his name. But his exceptional batting skills were recognized after a chance hit during a net-practice session. His coach (Dinesh Lad) had been taken aback by the felicity with which the little fella wielded the willow. Thus began his tilt at glory.

Rohit might not be acknowledged as Destiny's Child like Dhoni and Mohammad Azharuddin before, but various forces united at different points in his career to give him the opportunity to showcase his abilities, which he utilized to the hilt to reach where he is today.

Victory at the 2024 Men's T20 World Cup might have ended a long trophy drought as far as India is concerned, but for Rohit, it is far from the end of the journey. There are more peaks to scale, many other lands and tournaments to conquer. Rohit isn't the sort to live in the past. Those closest to him insist, with an indulgent smile, that the present too can confound him sometimes—he often spaces out even in the middle of a sentence. But he has shown that he is adept at learning lessons from history to emerge a better cricketer every single day. From the long early years of international uncertainty to becoming one of the all-time great white-ball batters and an efficient and combative Test opener in the last several years is a tribute to Rohit's self-belief and work ethic, traits that have often been overshadowed by his incandescent batsmanship.

Prologue

Winning the World Cup

He lay on the ground, belly-down. His right hand slapped the turf furiously in a display of raw emotion from a man who can be demonstrative when he wants to be, though generally in a nice, fun-filled, bantering fashion.

But this was something else.

This was an outpouring of pent-up sentiment—great elation and unmatched delight, of course. But also relief.

Huge relief.

It's unlikely that the dismaying turn of events from seven and a half months back would not have flitted through his mind at that time. It is often during the most glorious moments that the darkness of the past resurfaces—unexpected and unwanted. The pall of gloom that had descended over Ahmedabad *that* night, however, had been emphatically exploded. Rohit Sharma was a World Cup winner all over again. But this time there was a difference. A massive difference.

He was the captain of a World Cup-winning outfit; only the third man—after Kapil Dev and Mahendra Singh Dhoni—to take his country all the way to the title, and just the second—after Dhoni—to carry his team to the *Promised Land* in the T20 version. Rohit was due some emotion, wasn't he?

Defeat to Australia in the final of the 50-over World Cup on 19 November 2023 had stung badly. India had mounted just about the perfect campaign until then, overcoming the pre-tournament loss of Axar Patel and the mid-event injury-enforced departure of ace all-rounder Hardik Pandya. Propelled by their inspirational captain who walked the talk and took aggression during Powerplay to new heights, India were an unstoppable force after overcoming early hiccups to muscle past Australia in their opener in Chennai. By the final, they were ticking along beautifully, an amalgam of grace and power, of fearsome intent and immaculate execution.

Nearly a hundred thousand people at the Narendra Modi Stadium were convinced that it was India's time. Rohit's time. But it wasn't to be. India didn't quite measure up to scratch when it came to the crunch. The knockout bogey struck again, like it repeatedly had since the 2014 T20 World Cup in Bangladesh. There was no fairytale end to the riveting journey; instead of triumph and celebration, the Sunday night ended in agony and unchecked tears.

Few get the opportunity to sing the redemption song and fewer still get the chance to do so as quickly after such a gargantuan heartbreak. That's what the six-wicket defeat in Ahmedabad was to millions of Indians, to every member of the squad that exhilarated through the tournament, but especially to the skipper who had left no stone unturned in his quest for ultimate glory. He hurt badly in the immediate aftermath of

Prologue: Winning the World Cup

the loss. It took him a long, long time to push it to the deep recesses of his memory because, in his own words, 'life has to go on'. Assignments came one after another—a Test tour of South Africa, a return to Twenty20 Internationals in the home series against Afghanistan after a 14-month absence, a draining five-Test showdown against England, and Season 17 of the Indian Premier League where, for the first time since 2014, he wouldn't start as the captain of his franchise.

Rohit tore through these trials with narrow focus, though his eye was on the larger picture of the T20 World Cup to be jointly hosted by the United States—hitherto only accustomed to staging the occasional high-ticket international—and the West Indies. As he enjoyed one of his better recent editions with the bat during the IPL, Rohit kept a lookout for signs that would allow him and his head coach Rahul Dravid to help Ajit Agarkar's selection panel nail down the one or two positions in the national squad that had multiple contenders. Even as five-time champions Mumbai Indians crashed and burned under new skipper Pandya, India were silently assembling a crack outfit that would give them the best chance to reprise the magic of 2007 under Dhoni. There can't be another Dhoni, needless to say. But Rohit is his own man—a leader in so many ways even before he became India's all-format captain in early 2022, a shrewd tactician and an excellent man-manager. But, most importantly, he is a man bereft of that damaging, self-defeating type of ego.

They say that some ego is an essential trait in any creative artist. It fuels the pursuit of excellence and the quest to go where few have gone before; it's this quality that drives one to

The Rise of the Hitman

aspire for the sky and beyond. It stokes pride in performance, catalyzes the hunger to script a legacy, lay down the marker and act as an inspiration for future generations. Perhaps what they say is not true. Maybe you can get there even without any ego. But it can't hurt, can it?

Rohit's ego, if any, was restricted to his batsmanship—beautifully brutal, making even the odd crude hoick appear aesthetically appealing. Beyond that, he was the benevolent older brother to the younger lads in the team and an equal to the not-so-inexperienced virtuosos, like Virat Kohli, Jasprit Bumrah, Ravindra Jadeja and Pandya. An individual can't win everything on their own in a team setting, though there have been geniuses across disciplines who might have appeared to do so. Rohit's great gift is in his ability to bring everyone together. He didn't need to get everyone on the same page because they already were—just as desperate as their leader to be known as world champions, as World Cup winners. Rohit's task, along with Dravid, was to ensure that they didn't start working subconsciously at cross-purposes in that desperation.

India's campaign at the T20 World Cup wasn't as dominant as it had been in its 50-over counterpart a few months prior. But fittingly, they were the only unbeaten team when the dust settled. Conditions at the Nassau Country International Cricket Stadium in New York, where they played their first three matches, prevented India from rustling up the momentum they would have liked. However, there was satisfaction aplenty in having conquered the conditions just as well as the three opponents, among them old friends and World Cup bunnies Pakistan.

Prologue: Winning the World Cup

There is something to be said for steamrolling oppositions, but hard-fought victories do wonders for morale and confidence. India defended 119 against Pakistan expertly—with some help from Babar Azam's men, but largely because they weren't willing to settle for second-best. With Bumrah in spectacular form, they bore down on Pakistan with all their might, sticking to their disciplines and refusing to panic even when the game seemed to be slipping away, and gathering force like a wrecking ball once the well-set Mohammad Rizwan threw them a lifeline.

Great units wait for that one opportunity—a little opening that can be stepped into and built upon. They are adept at seizing the moment. That is exactly what India did time and again in the World Cup, not least in the 29 June final against South Africa at the Kensington Oval in beautiful Bridgetown. They had provided a preview earlier in the tournament when they sensed they had a sniff and ferociously charged at Pakistan, blowing the middle and lower orders away, not with naked aggression but astute assurance. India's composure was in stark contrast to Pakistan's leaden feet and heavy heads, no doubt crammed with the baggage of past World Cup losses. Once their favourite World Cup rivals were taken care of, there was the small matter of making it to the knockout semifinals—even though the Super Eights were their next assignment.

That might appear a little presumptuous, given that the immediate target for a team in any competition is to get out of each stage unscathed. Nothing is as straightforward as it seems in sports, Pakistan's elimination from Group A after their stunning Super Over loss to the United States being a shining

The Rise of the Hitman

example of the glorious uncertainties. But, while they wouldn't have taken their progression to the Super Eights for granted, India would have fancied going through as one of two teams from a five-team pool where the other two were Ireland and Canada. For United States, a place in the Super Eight stage was a victory in itself; for India, it was the first step in a journey that had just started.

The move from the dodgy surfaces of New York, and the washout against Canada in Lauderhill, to the Caribbean where the pitches were far better—if not the shirtfronts that the IPL threw up unfailingly in 2024—energized India's batters. Rohit and Kohli—united as openers in a bid to maximize the latter's sensational form during the IPL—didn't always fire in unison, but the middle order was in supreme touch. India made smart alterations—smart because they paid off, perhaps?—to their batting order, taking cues from the Total Football of the 1970s in Europe, and assigned different roles to different individuals in different matches, or even at different stages of the same match. This carried an element of surprise—sometimes even for the batter who was promoted, such as Axar who batted at number five in the final—which made planning for scenarios difficult and pushed teams out of their comfort zones. India won the title as much with their planning as their execution and, as those who know him will affirm, Rohit is nothing if not a meticulous planner.

The decision to plump for Shivam Dube ahead of Rinku Singh, for example, was devoid of sentiment or emotion. Rinku has made a name for himself in the last few seasons as a consummate finisher, but in that same period, Dube has established himself as an acknowledged slayer of spin. True, his medium pace gave the team an additional bowling option—Dube was one of four all-rounders, alongside Pandya, Jadeja and Axar—but it was in his takedown of spin that the strapping Mumbaikar was in his element. He didn't disappoint, reining in his aggression when India were in a bit of trouble against United States in New York but rediscovering his six-hitting mojo in the Caribbean where his little cameos added up to a lot in the final analysis.

For all their batting firepower—and India had plenty, including Suryakumar Yadav—the bowling needed to stand up. Rohit will be the first to put his hand up and gratefully acknowledge the impact of Bumrah, the deserved Player of the Tournament, for landing telling punches at the most opportune moments. Such was the threat carried by the pacer from Gujarat that oppositions started to believe that they only had 16 overs to bat instead of 20. Bumrah's four were earmarked for survival, but that precaution didn't prevent him from picking up 15 wickets. The most runs he conceded in a match were 29—ridiculous, considering that between them, India and Australia amassed 386 runs in 40 overs—and his overall economy for the tournament was an extraordinary 4.17 from 29.4 overs spread across eight matches. But, as stratospheric as these numbers are, they can't even begin to quantify the influence he had on the tournament.

Bumrah didn't plough a lone furrow—Arshdeep Singh was an able understudy, ending up with a joint tournament-high 17 wickets, Kuldeep Yadav was mesmeric from the moment he was unleashed in the Super Eights until South Africa laid

The Rise of the Hitman

into him in the final, and Axar was quite the unsung hero, backing his crucial batting contributions with stunning spells of left-arm spin as he usurped the senior spinning all-rounder status from Jadeja. Pandya—fresh off a forgettable stint in the IPL, as both captain and player—also came into his own as the World Cup unspooled. His wicket of Heinrich Klaasen in the seventeenth over of the final was the first of numerous crucial developments that inexorably altered the destination of the trophy.

India's all-win Super Eight record gave them the chance to atone for their loss in the previous T20 World Cup with another semifinal against England—a match that promised much but fizzled out into a one-sided romp. Although Jos Buttler stuck to his guns, insisting that his decision to chase was the right one, India weren't complaining; not after amassing 171 for seven on a Providence surface where the ball was turning square and batting first was by far the better proposition.

Like he had done against Australia a few days before—lashing a decisive 92 runs off 41 balls—Rohit again led from the front with 57 off 39. The Australia knock was particularly vital because it put India's World Cup bugbears out of the tournament and reaffirmed the belief within the team that their time in the sun was imminent. And once they had posted 171, scoring more than 8.5 runs per over, with spinners ripping it past the bat, the target was next to impossible for England. They keeled over for 103, leaving a 68-run margin that almost mirrored England's ten-wicket hammering of India in the previous semifinal in Adelaide in 2022.

While India were the dominant and eyeball-attracting

behemoth—all their scheduled matches and the potential semifinal and final being earmarked for a 10.30 a.m. local time-slot (8.00 p.m. in India) to facilitate prime-time viewing back home—South Africa carved their way through the field in equally emphatic fashion, raising hopes of ending three decades of World Cup heartbreaks, dating back to their 1992 debut in the 50-over edition. Aiden Markram ran a tight ship—the middle order was bristling with talent, the pace attack was formidable with Kagiso Rabada and the express Anrich Nortje operating on a different plane, and the two left-arm spinners, the orthodox Keshav Maharaj and the wrist-spinner Tabraiz Shamsi, complementing each other superbly.

Would the perennial bridesmaids finally shed that unenviable tag? Or would India wear the crown again?

The final was tense and frenetic, yo-yoing this way and that, until the decisive five overs when India became unstoppable, their desperation trumping their rivals'. Kohli shed a terrible trot with a match-winning 76 that helped him double his previous tally in the tournament, but it could just as easily not have been—such was the thin line between agony and ecstasy. Once again, the value of runs on the board in a cup final became evident; though, had South Africa held their nerve and had India not been so switched on in the last eighth of the final, there could have been a different tale to tell.

Those last five overs were a spectacle on their own, not just the climactic conclusion to a larger battle. Through Quinton de Kock, Tristan Stubbs, David Miller and the irrepressible Klaasen, South Africa had made light of the early dismissals of Reeza Hendricks and Markram in their quest for the 177 that

The Rise of the Hitman

would have made years of meltdowns and horrible fortune worth it. After 15 overs, the score was 147 for four, Klaasen taking Kuldeep and Axar apart; 30 needed off 30 balls, six wickets in hand. If Rohit's face didn't mirror his worst fears, it was only because the thick foliage on his visage masked his tension. On the surface, he was calm and in control, unshaken by imminent defeat.

He had one ace up his sleeve which he unleashed before it was too late. Bumrah's third over, the 16th of the chase, didn't produce a wicket, but it only went for four runs and returned a semblance of balance and stability after Axar had leaked 24 in the previous one. As always, the smiling assassin had kept his team afloat, but India needed wickets. 26 off 24 was a walk in the park with a belligerent Klaasen and a marauding Miller in the middle. What do you do, Rohit?

What do you do?

Rohit turned to his deputy, the man with whom he had an allegedly fractious relationship after the Mumbai Indians captaincy saga. Throughout the tournament, there had been little indication of any friction between Rohit and Pandya, but that didn't stop wagging tongues, whispers, innuendos and less couched suggestions that all was not well between them.

Balderdash!

Pandya is the kind of player who makes things happen. Admittedly, the manner of Klaasen's dismissal wasn't part of the script—but hey, a wicket at that stage? India took it gladly, however it came.

It came off a slow, wide off-cutter that Klaasen—perhaps losing concentration after the long pause in play spent tending

Prologue: Winning the World Cup

to comeback hero Rishabh Pant's troublesome knee—reached out for with a wild waft. The ball caught the edge of the bat on its way to the keeper's mitts.

Kensington Oval erupted in applause! Now India were energized.

Kohli snarled, Rohit screamed in delight, and hands were thrown up in jubilation.

Hang on—you wanted to yell—it's still 26 runs off 23 balls with five wickets in hand. What are you so gung-ho about?

But they knew, didn't they? They knew what they were capable of, where their belief would lead. They knew they could force the gap open and break the door down, strangling South Africa with their aggression and stoking those gremlins of self-doubt.

They knew...

Bumrah cleaned up Marco Jansen—his last resounding statement in a tournament full of them—and Arshdeep, cool as ice, conceded four in the nineteenth over.

Pandya to Miller, 16 off six deliveries—the World Cup on the line. After four weeks and 54 matches, it had come down to the last four or so minutes.

Rohit and Pandya took their time setting the field, moving fielders around like pieces on a chessboard, making sure the high-traffic areas were properly manned. So, there was Kohli at long-on to the left-hander and Suryakumar a million yards to his right, at long-off.

Nearly a million yards is what Suryakumar ran to his left to complete one of the more special catches in a final. *Any* final. It drew comparisons with Kapil Dev's catch that dismissed

The Rise of the Hitman

Viv Richards in the 1983 World Cup final—'Let it be, *yaar*,' Rohit drawled later—and why would it not? Miller lashed a wide full toss outside off that seemed destined to land beyond the ropes and bring the equation down to a more manageable 10 off five when Suryakumar ran like the wind, his eyes unwaveringly on the ball, his assured feet eating up the ground. More than anything else, his mind sized up the situation under immense pressure—just to hold the catch was a magnificent effort. To have the awareness of where his feet were with regard to the boundary buntings, to have the smarts to toss the ball up, then waltz back in and retake the catch was little short of miraculous. After a cursory look at the replays, because that's all that was required, TV umpire Richard Kettleborough flashed OUT on the giant screen. A billion Indians, including the 11 in the middle of Kensington Oval, roared as one; that was the moment when the final breath whooshed out of the South African chase.

The last five deliveries couldn't be a blur, they weren't a formality. The biggest threat was gone, but T20 games have a life of their own, right? Wrong. Pandya was businesslike—no-nonsense and in the zone. There was a wide, yes, but also the wicket of Rabada, this time caught without fuss by Suryakumar walking in from long-off. And then the perfect last ball with nine required, one that Nortje could only bunt to deep mid-wicket for a single.

Pandya, drained, sank to the ground, still in a daze. Kohli threw his hands up as he looked heavenwards, sporting a beatific smile. The rest charged to the middle, where they hoped to find their captain, sprinting for a souvenir stump. Instead, Rohit lay

Prologue: Winning the World Cup

on the ground at cover, hammering the turf with the right hand that he has seldom used as a battering ram despite his penchant for sixes. He was now a World Cup-winning captain. Greatest achievement as a leader? Till date, yes, he will reply, with that infectious smile. Take a bow, Captain Fantastic.

1
Humble Beginnings

Any pursuit in the early years of life is influenced by one of three factors—curiosity, peer pressure, or the pure joy the exercise provides. Rohit Sharma got into cricket because that was the thing to do when he was growing up, especially in a city like Mumbai which was a dominant cricketing force at the time, with stars abound in every part of the bustling metropolis.

In that bygone era, kids didn't necessarily get into cricket with the intention of playing for the country. Times have changed and today there is a greater focus on the pathway to the future. The national team might not be the ultimate destination for many—many of the parents, that is. Maybe the T20 bug has bitten them so hard that the Indian Premier League is the preferred option now. After all, the IPL can accommodate close to 200 Indian cricketers while the national team is an entirely different beast. Coaching too wasn't as organized as it is today.

But as they say, where there is a will there is a way. Sachin Tendulkar's move from his parents' home to his uncle and aunt's home in the quest to hone his skills under Dronacharya Ramakant Achrekar is legendary. Rohit's journey wasn't the same, although there is the commonality of him living with his uncle and aunt (and grandmother) rather than his parents during his formative years.

Rohit's father, who worked in a transport company, decided to move his family from Borivali, in the west, to Dombivli, a distant Central Mumbai suburb. That didn't cut ice with Rohit's grandmother, who insisted that the first grandchild of the extended family should stay with her and her younger son in Borivali. Once the matriarch had spoken, there was no scope for arguments or debates, though financial considerations also played a significant part in the final decision. So, Rohit's father Gurunath, mother Purnima and younger brother Vishal shifted to Dombivli, while Rohit stayed put. This decision was to have a significant say in how his career would eventually pan out. After all, there is no knowing what course events would have taken if he had also gone to Dombivli with his parents.

'We played in our building, in the society. There is a shortage of space in Bombay. You just had to manage with whatever you have,' Rohit had said on Jitendra Chouksey's YouTube channel in September 2024.* 'I started playing with all my friends, school friends at times. Building friends are with whom I played for fun. I never knew it would become like this.

'The sport has got so many demands, be it travelling, learning the skills, fitness, training. In Mumbai, if you want to

---

*Chouksey, Jitendra, 'In conversation with Rohit Sharma', *YouTube*, 28 September 2024, https://tinyurl.com/mtc3kcf7, Accessed on 19 February 2025.

be a cricketer, you have to travel—two hours of travelling by train, five to six hours of playing, then travelling back—(and) you do not know whether you will get a seat. It did take a toll on me physically and mentally. But I enjoyed that, and those hard yards made me tough. That is what made me (what I am) today and helps make tough decisions these days.'

Rohit's uncle enrolled him in the Borivali Sports and Cultural Association when he was only 12, a move that would hugely influence his career path. It was while playing for the BSCA team in one of the many summer tournaments in 1999 that he caught the eye of Dinesh Lad, now a renowned coach, who was then with the Swami Vivekananda International School. His first tryst with Rohit impressed Lad so much that he met Rohit's uncle and told him that if Rohit was seriously interested in embracing the sport as a potential career, he must consider shifting to Lad's school. But it wasn't Rohit's batting that had caught the coach's discerning eye.

In one of those strange but true tales, Lad was taken in by Rohit's off-spin—the nice, easy and fluid action, the good loop and the impeccable control for one so young. 'My school was playing against the BSCA team in the final of the Under-12 section, and we were chasing less than 70 in a ten-over game,' Lad recalls. 'I don't remember much about the first half of the match, I am not even sure if I saw Rohit bat. But when he came on to bowl, I sat up and took notice. He bowled only 12 deliveries, but that was enough to make a deep impression on me.'

The Swami Vivekananda International School in Gorai had been founded by Yogesh Patel in 1995. It was still in its infancy and in Rohit, Lad saw someone who could make its fledgling cricket team stronger. At the end of the final, he approached the lad, keen to meet his guardian. Fortunately, Rohit's uncle had come to watch the match, so the coach approached him and offered his nephew a seat in his school. 'Once he agreed, I got the form filled and took it to Mr Patel (the director-cum-owner), impressing upon him the value Rohit would add to our cricket team. He immediately agreed to bring Rohit on board, but that wasn't the end of the story.'

At that point of time, Rohit was studying in Our Lady of Velankanni High School, where the monthly fee was ₹30. At SVIS, he would have to pay nine times more than that—₹275/month. 'Once his uncle came to know this, he told me that Rohit couldn't join the school,' Lad points out. 'He said the family couldn't afford to pay that amount each month just for Rohit's school fees, their financial situation didn't allow them that luxury. I understood their predicament, but I was also keen to have Rohit in SVIS, so I went back to the director and requested him to treat Rohit as a special case and waive the school fees. He was kind enough to oblige, and that's how Rohit eventually joined our school as a seventh-grade student. Who knows what might have happened had the director not been generous in bringing Rohit to our school without him having to pay the fees.' Long before the cricketing world learnt about Rohit Sharma, he had already created history by becoming the first student in the history of his school to be given a freeship—the waiver of school fees.

Success didn't come instantly; the climb up the rungs wasn't dramatic and immediate. The school team wasn't among

Humble Beginnings

the strongest and practice facilities were quite limited. The initial focus was on the Under-16 team playing the Harris Shield; once that was out of the way, the attention turned to the Under-14 team that Rohit was a part of, which played the Giles Shield but lost early in the competition. That was it for 1999 as far as cricket was concerned.

The following year, Lad promoted Rohit to the Under-16 team while also retaining him in the Under-14 squad. One day, as he was making his way towards the school gate, Lad noticed a batter knocking and was entranced by the straightness of the bat and the timing of his strokes. 'I had no idea who this boy was until I went closer and saw that it was Rohit. I didn't know he could bat, let alone bat so beautifully,' Lad says, his erstwhile disbelief manifesting itself in wistfulness. 'I asked him if he batted too and he said a little shyly, "*thoda kar leta hoon,* sir; I manage a bit". Till then, I had thought of him only as a very promising off-spinner because even when he was in BSCA, he had voluntarily chosen bowling. But I realized that—as good as his off-spin was—I couldn't ignore the fact that he had the skills to be an even better batter than a bowler.'

Thus, Rohit's batting career was born. In his first outing at number three in the Harris Shield that year, he chimed in with a 40, which earned him a promotion to the top of the order for the Giles Shield in 2000. He responded with a 140, justifying his coach's faith in him and driving Lad to spend hours with the young lad on the cement track at school. Lad hurled a new ball at him from 16 yards and was fascinated at how effortlessly the pull stroke came to his young charge. 'He was a natural. I didn't have to teach him to play the pull. He had the talent, his basics were strong, he was technically very sound even from an early age, and that's why he has been able to thrive in Test cricket too,' Lad asserts. 'My only contribution to his batting was giving him the opportunity to open the innings.'

As Rohit's batting exploits mounted, he began to attract the attention of the who's who of Mumbai Cricket. There is a strong network of cricket enthusiasts in the city. They share information and inputs, alerting each other to the presence of possible future stars. This network involves the entire cricketing fraternity—coaches, yes, but also scorers and umpires and ground staff, not to mention fans who would largely turn up in their own localities and exchange notes with friends and colleagues. By 15, Rohit was scoring runs for fun and it was inevitable that he would grab the attention of the sport's diaspora.

By the time he was in tenth grade, Rohit was bossing schools' cricket; that year alone, he made nearly 15 hundreds. People were slowly beginning to take notice of his prodigious talent. The Kalpesh Koli tournament was an audition to pick Under-16 probables and even though he was picked to play for the Borivali Centre, Rohit didn't get a single game because the coach plumped for a similar type of player—a batter-cum-off-spinner.

But, as they say, when one door closes another opens. In Rohit's case, that happened when the Board of Control for Cricket in India (BCCI) modified its Under-16 tournament to an Under-17 event the following year, making him eligible for selection all over again. The Kalpesh Koli tournament was the inevitable stepping stone, with the Player of the Tournament award sealing his place—first, in the Mumbai Under-17 probables, and then in the state side for the West Zone Under-17 competition for the 2003 Vijay Merchant Trophy.

'Rohit didn't get to play the first few games,' Lad says. 'I even spoke to the coach of the side, the great Vasu Paranjape sir, who acknowledged Rohit's talent but said that he had to bide his time. Fortunately for Rohit, one of the batters got injured midway through the competition. He got his chance against Saurashtra and made 60, batting in the middle order (at number five; incidentally, Ajinkya Rahane was one of the openers for Mumbai). He made it to the West Zone Under-17 camp and eventually to the India Under-17 team that played the Asia Cup in Bengaluru in January 2004.'

A little later that year, Rohit had his first taste of 'senior' nets with the Mumbai squad. 'There are certain things that just stick in your memory, that you always remember,' observes Ajit Agarkar, the former Indian pacer who is now the chairman of the Senior Men's Selection Committee. 'You know, as happens in Mumbai cricket, you're always told there's another batter coming through. I remember we were practising at the Cricket Club of India and Mr Dilip Vengsarkar was the chairman of the selection committee. Rohit had been called in to bat and I remember many people saying—when he came into bat—that this is the next guy, the next potential superstar batter coming through.

'I am sure he was a bit nervous. I remember bowling to him a little bit in the nets and the one thing that struck me even at that point was that he wasn't hurried. He seemed to have a little bit more time and you can sometimes just make out a player. When you're coming into the Ranji nets, especially as someone so young, there are some decent bowlers bowling at you and you perhaps haven't played at that level yet. But he looked… I mean, he might have gotten beaten or nicked off a few times, but he didn't look out of place at all. That's how I remember my first meeting with Rohit; that was sort of my first experience of him.'

The decision to stay in Borivali, even if he had no say in the matter, was beginning to pay off. By making it to the state side and then the national team, if only at the Under-17 level, Rohit had taken the first little steps towards realizing his dream of becoming the player he wanted to be.

2

The Early Promise

A little over a month after the Vijay Merchant Trophy, India hosted the Under-17 Asia Cup at the M. Chinnaswamy Stadium in Bengaluru in January 2004. Rohit had done enough for the state side to warrant selection, though the tournament wasn't very memorable for him. He didn't get to bat in the first three league games—which India won easily—and made 17 in the final which Pakistan clinched comfortably by six wickets. Leggie Piyush Chawla and left-arm spinner Shahbaz Nadeem, both of whom would go on to play Test cricket, were the lead spinners. Thus, Rohit's off-spin wasn't called into action at all. As far as international debuts go, this was particularly underwhelming.

Better tidings were in store when Rohit returned to Bengaluru for the KSCA MRF Trophy two-day matches in August 2004. He was picked to represent the National Cricket Academy, housed at Chinnaswamy, and it was there that he wowed a wider audience. Against strong bowling attacks, he made 120, 17, 88 and 38 to play a significant part in the youngsters' march to the semifinals, where they succumbed to ONGC by two wickets. His century had come against Air India, and former India batter Pravin Amre was so fascinated by the 17-year-old's striking batsmanship that he immediately offered Rohit a scholarship from Air India.

Within a couple of months, he was fast-tracked to the Under-19s, representing Mumbai in the Vinoo Mankad Trophy and the Cooch Behar Trophy, and West Zone in the Vijay Hazare Trophy. Clearly, this was a star on the rise and it came as no surprise when, in February 2005, he made his India Under-19 debut in a three-match 50-over series at home against England. Despite not setting the house on fire, he was picked for the subsequent five-match faceoff with Australia, also at home. Against a quality attack that included Jackson Bird, among others, Rohit was consistent even if the big scores proved elusive. He opened the batting in the final game in Delhi and by the end of the series—which India won—it was clear that he would be on the plane to Colombo in February 2006 as one of the batting lynchpins at the Under-19 World Cup.

Rohit lived up to that billing, emerging as India's third highest run-maker, behind openers Cheteshwar Pujara and Gaurav Dhiman. He made three half-centuries in six innings but was one of seven top-order batters to be dismissed for a single-digit score as India were shot out for 71 and went down to Pakistan by 38 runs in a low-scoring final. For the second time in a little over two years, Rohit had been at the receiving end of a loss to Pakistan in the final of a major age-group tournament. By the time Rohit graduated to the senior ranks,

The Early Promise

India already boasted an impressive World Cup record against Pakistan and he ensured that that record would be extended across formats, the only blip being a ten-wicket loss at the Dubai T20 World Cup in 2021.

Less than a week after the shattering loss in the Colombo final, Rohit made his senior representative debut for West Zone in the 50-over Deodhar Trophy against Central Zone on 25 February 2006. He was one of three debutants for West, alongside his World Cup teammates Pujara and Ravindra Jadeja. Who knew then that these three would go on to form the backbone of the Indian team one day?

On debut in Gwalior, Rohit was slotted in at number eight and walked in with his side in serious trouble, at 97 for six chasing Central's 180. There was pressure all right, but this was also a great opportunity for the 18-year-old to showcase his mettle. The required rate was not a big factor, so Rohit could afford to take his time, and that's precisely what he did. Showcasing maturity well beyond his years, he stabilized the tottering innings with a stand of 44 for the seventh wicket with Bhavik Thaker. When the latter was bowled by Piyush Chawla, West still required 40 runs; Rohit found another ally in the left-handed Jadeja and West got home by three wickets with four overs to spare, Rohit's contribution in the victory a measured 31 not out off 47 deliveries.

So impressed was skipper Parthiv Patel with the young man's temperament and skill that he elevated Rohit to number three for West's next outing against a formidable North Zone side in Udaipur. Gautam Gambhir scored a hundred and put on 134 for the first wicket with Shikhar Dhawan to justify

Dinesh Mongia's decision to bat, North finishing at 278 for nine when they ran out of overs. It ought to have been a testing run-chase until Rohit made it singularly one-sided with a blazing unbeaten 142 off just 123 deliveries. North had a high-quality bowling attack—Gagandeep Singh, Joginder Sharma, Reetinder Singh Sodhi, Abid Nabi and Amit Mishra—but Rohit ripped into the line-up without mercy, smashing 14 fours and three sixes. Parthiv's masterstroke had struck paydirt and Rohit was in business.

Inching towards the Big Leagues

Rohit had gone from being a promising talent to a batter on the verge of bigger things. His skills had convinced the authorities to look onwards and upwards, and his call-up to the India A team for the first time in April 2006—to play against the A teams of Pakistan, Ireland and United Arab Emirates at the newly inaugurated Sheikh Zayed Stadium in Abu Dhabi—was an organic development. His batting in the Deodhar Trophy, his first senior competition, was enough for the national selectors to want to test him out against bowling of a higher quality and Rohit was again in his element, carving out half-centuries in his first two knocks even though there was a familiar disappointment in the final against Pakistan.

It was evident that unless things went horribly wrong, it was only a matter of time before he was fast-tracked into the Indian limited-overs teams. He was still in his teens but was clearly a cut above most of his contemporaries, and pushing for a spot in the middle order despite the presence of such stalwarts as Rahul

The Early Promise

Dravid, Yuvraj Singh and Mahendra Singh Dhoni. Further proof that he had risen in the pecking order came with his selection to the India A team that travelled to Australia that July for the Top End Series which also included the developmental squads of the host nation, Pakistan and New Zealand.

His first-class debut was a few months away, by which time he had made his debut in the Challenger Series for the NKP Salve Trophy. At the time, it was a three-team tournament that featured the cream of the country's talent; Rohit's inclusion in the India Red squad cemented the widely-held belief that his international debut was imminent.

Rohit's maiden Ranji Trophy appearance for Mumbai was in December 2006, against Bengal at the Eden Gardens. Although he would make pleasant memories at the stadium going forward, this first match was anything but memorable. The multiple-time champions conceded a massive first-innings lead. Nine wicketless overs were followed by a modest 21 before he was dismissed by off-spinner Saurasish Lahiri, and he didn't get to bat when Mumbai followed on. It wasn't the strongest Mumbai side, with several stalwarts away on India duty in South Africa. Nonetheless, he had taken another step in the right direction.

His destiny was in his own hands now.

A busy season culminated with his List A and T20 debuts for Mumbai in the Vijay Hazare Trophy and the inaugural Syed Mushtaq Ali Trophy, respectively. By the time of his entry into the 20-over state side, India had crashed out of the 50-over World Cup in the Caribbean, in March 2007. The aftershocks would be seismic, with Greg Chappell bowing out as the head coach and Ravi Shastri stepping in on an interim basis for India's next international assignment against Bangladesh in May. India were to play two Tests and three One-Day Internationals. Rohit and Dinesh Lad both felt that his time had come and that he would be presented with a belated birthday (April 30) gift.

International Debut

'Two days before the squad was to be announced, a couple of television channels came to interview us,' Lad chuckles. 'I tried telling them not to jump the gun, to wait for the announcement of the team, but they said there was no chance Rohit would not be picked. We were both delighted but unfortunately, when the team was named, Rohit missed out, with the nod going to Manoj Tiwary (the Bengal batter). To say that Rohit was very upset would be an understatement, but I reminded him that he was still only 20, had a long career ahead of him, and must derive inspiration from the fact that he was already in the reckoning to break into a strong Indian side.'

India were hugely in demand then—as they are now—and, not long after the Bangladesh tour, were slated to travel to Ireland, Scotland and then England, where they would play three Tests and seven ODIs. 'Like a few years back when the Under-16 BCCI tournament was modified to an Under-17 tournament and allowed Rohit to make his mark, luck favoured him here too,' Lad observes. 'Manoj sadly hurt his shoulder in Bangladesh, which perhaps facilitated Rohit's selection. He only played one (or) two international matches on that entire tour, but he was now an India player!'

The Early Promise

Rohit had been picked for the Irish and Scottish legs where India would play five ODIs—one each against the two host nations and three against South Africa for the Future Cup in Belfast. Rohit's debut came in the first match itself, against Ireland, in Belfast on 23 June 2007. Among his teammates were Sourav Ganguly, his hero Sachin Tendulkar, Gambhir, and Yuvraj and Dinesh Karthik, with both of whom Rohit would go on to strike terrific friendships. These stalwarts were led by Rahul Dravid. To say that he was overwhelmed to occupy the same dressing-room as all of them would be another understatement; to be on the same field, rubbing shoulders, was an even more exhilarating and nervy experience.

Rohit didn't get to do a great deal in his first match, apart from registering his first international catch to dismiss Niall O'Brien, the Irish keeper. India hunted down Ireland's 193 with consummate ease, winning by nine wickets with Ganguly and Gambhir putting on 162 for the second wicket. Pencilled in at number seven, Rohit didn't even need to don his pads. While that was disappointing, it still couldn't dampen the thrill of wearing the India cap.

Three days later, he would bat in an international game for the first time against South Africa at the same Civil Service Cricket Club at Stormont in Belfast. He lasted nine deliveries, making eight runs, before becoming the first of two victims for Jacques Kallis. 'His first outing with the bat in the middle, interestingly, was with me,' reflects Karthik. 'I was at the non-striker's end when he walked in. Yuvi had just been dismissed by Andrew Hall and Rohit asked me how he was bowling. I told him that he was bowling very fast and that I was not able to pick his action either. Perhaps that played a part in his dismissal, I am not sure.

'What I do know is that he kept the incident in his mind for a long time. When we went out to dinner nearly a decade later, he was telling his wife, "I don't know what mistake I made in life to have him as my first batting partner (for India). I was playing my first match, international debut, I asked him how the bowler was bowling and he says I don't know, he is bowling fast and I can't pick his action. All the inputs were negative and he put the fear inside me." That was my first interaction with him. It didn't start on the best note, I didn't give him enough confidence. But we have obviously come a long way since then.'

Rohit sat out the next two games against the Proteas and the one-off game against Scotland was rained out. Rohit's tour was over for the time being.

While the Test team was engaged in a stirring battle with the English—India won a series in England for the first time since 1986—Rohit was on the flight to Harare as part of the India A squad for two four-day games against a Zimbabwe Select XI and one against Kenya A in Mombasa. Again, without hogging the headlines, he showcased decent touch and rejoined the Indian team for the seven ODIs in England, though, to his great frustration, all he did was ferry drinks.

The Other World Cup

Amidst the disappointment came the silver lining—he was in a young, inexperienced and unprepossessing 15, to be led by

The Early Promise

first-time captain Dhoni, at the inaugural T20 World Cup in South Africa. Batting superstars Dravid, Tendulkar and Ganguly had made themselves unavailable.

The 20-over format itself was yet to fire the imagination of Indians. Furthermore, given their misadventures in the Caribbean, where India lost to Bangladesh and Sri Lanka and crashed out of the 50-over World Cup in the first stage itself, there were hardly any expectations back home when Dhoni's warriors landed in Johannesburg for the *other* World Cup.

At the 2007 T20 World Cup, matches that ended in a tie went to a 'bowl-out'. Each team had to designate five players who would bowl at a set of untenanted stumps to break the deadlock. It is not clear what routine the other teams followed, but India practised for bowl-outs at the nets; what's more, the coaching group of Lalchand Rajput, Venkatesh Prasad and Robin Singh kept scores, and of all the Indians, Rohit had the highest success rate when it came to hitting the stumps.

Yet, he could only watch on helplessly after India's group encounter with Pakistan in Durban ended in a tie, a game for which he was not picked. India won by a football-like scoreline of 3-0 after their first three bowlers—Harbhajan Singh, Virender Sehwag and Robin Uthappa—all hit the stumps and Pakistan's first three designated players were all off the mark. By now, Rohit's frustration was mounting and he called Lad with his favourite '*pak gaya*, sir' remark ('I am totally frustrated'). 'I told him to stay patient and bide his time,' Lad recalls.

His time came on 19 September, against England, at Kingsmead in Durban. But, like in his ODI debut, he didn't get to bat. He did, however, have a ringside view of Yuvraj's brutal assault on Stuart Broad that fetched him six sixes in an over and held a smart catch to get rid of opener Vikram Solanki, as India bounced back from the loss to New Zealand to register an 18-run win and keep their semifinal hopes alive. To get into the last four, India had to overcome hosts South Africa in their adoptive home of Durban.

Rohit's first Twenty20 International knock was far more memorable than his corresponding 50-over hit in Belfast. With Yuvraj indisposed, Rohit was thrust into the cauldron at 33 for three during the Powerplay. He responded with calm assurance and a distinct lack of nerves. His languid grace and easy bat-flow wowed the connoisseurs as he handled the typical liberal movement under the lights of Durban with aplomb against Shaun Pollock, Makhaya Ntini, Vernon Philander and Morne Morkel. Rohit and Dhoni added 85 for the fifth wicket in reasonably quick time, with the 20-year-old finishing on an unbeaten 50 off 40 deliveries—his maiden half-century in international cricket. That, allied with his run-out of the dangerous Justin Kemp, would bring him the first of numerous Player of the Match awards across formats.

'Even though our first on-field interaction got off to a rocky start, we connected straightaway,' Karthik smiles. 'And you just knew straightaway that he had the talent. By the T20 World Cup, we had got to a stage where we were good friends. We were talking, we'd go out for a meal on the odd day. I thought on the morning of the South Africa match that I'd be dropped, but I was still knocking when we got to the ground, like batters usually do on match-day.

'Rohit took the bat from me and hit a few balls and told

The Early Promise

me that the bat was really good. I thought I was going to be dropped and I didn't like that bat that much in any case, so I told him that he could keep it. He took the bat, changed the sticker and took it straight to the middle, without having had even a net with a stick he wasn't used to,' Karthik says, his expressive eyes opening wide. 'I was amazed that somebody could do something like that. He just took a bat and went straight into a World Cup match, where he was batting for the first time. I was out first ball, he got 50 not out! He said it was a lucky way to start with that bat. I'd always liked him as a person, I wanted him to do well on a personal note and in an oblique kind of way, I took delight in the fact that what was once my bat had played a part in his unbeaten half-century.'

After facing just a handful of deliveries during the semifinal victory over Australia, Rohit again walked in under pressure in the final—with just 28 deliveries left in the innings, India were 111 for four, and both Yuvraj and Dhoni were back in the hut. Rohit faced 16 balls in the last 4.4 overs, smashing two sixes on his way to 30 not out. Given what unfolded later in the match, it was a massive contribution, numerically the second highest in India's 157 after Gambhir's 75, but worth much more because it converted a middling total to a competitive one. The rest, as they say, is history. Within three months of his international debut, Rohit Sharma was a World Cup winner. Significantly, he had showcased his ability to thrive under pressure, to bat according to the situation, and to shift gears when required. For someone so young to take so quickly to the challenges of the sport at the highest level suggested a long and glorious career, provided he didn't take his eyes off the ball.

Lazy but Elegant

One of the first guys Rohit connected with in the Indian team was the mercurial left-hander Yuvraj Singh. 'I wouldn't say I took him under my wing, but we had a good equation,' Yuvraj reflects. 'I was a happy-go-lucky, fun-loving person, and so was Rohit. We kind of like gelled together quite a lot in terms of preparation and mindset.

'When he came into the side, he was a lazy guy, I would say,' Yuvraj continues. 'He was a supremely talented guy—very athletic, brilliant fielder, brilliant at coordination. But obviously, he was not someone who was very hard-working. He was like a very raw talent. But the more he saw the atmosphere of the team, where people go to the gym and recovery and all that, he got into that mode after a few years, as he got older. He's not someone who's been a very gym-friendly guy or someone who really focuses on diet. He's just a very naturally gifted sportsman. If I would have to compare him with somebody, it would have to be Inzamam-ul-Haq. Lazy but elegant. You always feel that guys like Rohit and Inzamam, when they're batting, they have so much extra time than others. Some people just are blessed with that kind of talent.'

Glimpses of Brilliance and Class: The 2007–08 Australia Tour

His career graph continued on an upward surge with further reiterations of his enormous talent coming during the tri-series in Australia. Early in the tournament, he guided India to a solid five-wicket win against the Aussies with a measured unbeaten 39. But the knock that caught everyone's eye came in the first of the best-of-three finals, also against the hosts, at the Sydney Cricket Ground.

India had never triumphed in a triangular series in Australia, and unsurprisingly, towards the end of a fractious tour, Ricky Ponting announced that the finals would end after just two games. They did, but not in a way that the Australian captain, or the rest of the cricketing world, would have envisaged.

The 2007–08 tour had been riddled with numerous controversies, peaking with the 'Monkeygate' episode when Andrew Symonds accused Harbhajan Singh of racial abuse. The Indian off-spinner was initially banned for three Tests by match referee Mike Procter, a ban that was overturned on appeal by Appeals Commissioner John Hansen. India had responded to the unsavoury events of Sydney, where they were also at the receiving end of at least a dozen poor umpiring decisions during the second Test, with a historic victory at the WACA ground in Perth in the succeeding Test. Victory in the tri-series would be the perfect riposte to the cocky Aussies.

What more fitting a place to pay the Aussies back than at the same venue where the tour threatened to devolve into a major diplomatic standoff? At the iconic SCG, India's bowlers did well to restrict the home side to 239 for eight, but the batters still had to get the job done. Tendulkar was in his element, playing some of the most gorgeous strokes of his outstanding career and wearing a steely determination that suggested that he was onto something special. But he needed support; Uthappa, Gambhir and Yuvraj made only 30 between them and at 87 for three, the match was in the balance.

In walked Rohit, the novelty of his brilliance replaced by

The Rise of the Hitman

the expectation from the dressing room that he was the real deal. More than once in his fledgling career he had showcased his comfort in playing with his back to the wall. How about once more, Rohit?

Why not, he seemed to say. Tendulkar was in subliminal touch when Rohit walked in, but even he was forced to play second fiddle as the young man found his bearings. The strokes came in a rush, but were unhurried—off the front foot and the back; on the off side and the legside; against the pace of Brett Lee and Nathan Bracken, and the fiery Mitchell Johnson and James Hopes; against the spin of Brad Hogg and Michael Clarke. But it wasn't just the big hits. Rohit's placement and judgement was impeccable as he engaged the man he idolized in a match-winning alliance of 123. By the time he was dismissed, he had danced his way to 66 and walked off to a standing ovation. Australia had had their first glimpse of Rohit, the multi-faceted destroyer.

Amidst the euphoria surrounding the partnership and the celebration of Rohit's class, Tendulkar sounded a note of caution. The Little Master, who sealed the chase with an unbeaten 117, was glowing in his praise of his young partner and predicted a bright future for his fellow Mumbaikar 'provided he keeps his head on his shoulders'. At the time, it was perceived as a typically guarded assessment by the senior statesman and no one thought much of it. However, for a brief while in the immediate future, the wisdom of those words would become apparent.

India won the first finals by six wickets and scraped out a nine-run win in the next game in Brisbane, proving Ponting ironically right. Their 2-0 sweep was their first significant

The Early Promise

silverware in Australia since the 1985 World Championship of Cricket crown in Melbourne. A 23-year wait had ended and the exploits of a certain 20-year-old had plenty to do with it.

By this time, Rohit had already been snapped up for a massive US$750,000 (₹4.8 crore) by Deccan Chargers in the inaugural IPL auction, which transpired during the tri-series. Memories of the early hardships in Borivali were fading to the deep recesses of Rohit's mind. He had arrived; in only nine months, he had made a name for himself in a team full of superstars. The world was at Rohit's feet; how he reacted to that in the next couple of years would determine what his legacy would be.

3

A Steady Climb, and Huge Setbacks

As India were creating history at the T20 World Cup in South Africa in September 2007, the Indian Premier League was announced with much fanfare back home. Conceptualized by Lalit Modi during his time in the United States in the 1990s and shot down more than a decade ago by the powers that be in the BCCI, the franchise-based T20 tournament came into existence after the board-unsanctioned, and subsequently defunct, Indian Cricket League had taken off.

One can only speculate how the IPL would have been received had India not emerged triumphant in South Africa. As it transpired, the success of Mahendra Singh Dhoni and his unfancied lads was just the shot in the arm the tournament needed even before a single ball was bowled. The BCCI had managed to attract the attention of the top players in the world, and the auction in February 2008, just a couple of months before the start of the maiden edition, was a huge draw, with cricketers being auctioned for the first time.

Rohit's early brilliance meant that he would be a hot

name at the auction. After much to and fro, Deccan Chargers won the 20-year-old's services. He hadn't come cheap, but no one had expected him to. Rohit's life had taken a dramatic upswing. But now, he had the weight of expectations on his broad shoulders to contend with.

The right-hander didn't disappoint in an otherwise miserable year for the Hyderabad-based outfit. Despite possessing the services of such overseas stalwarts as Herschelle Gibbs, Adam Gilchrist, Andrew Symonds and Shahid Afridi, Deccan Chargers mounted a forgettable campaign, winning just two of their 14 matches and bringing up the rear with four measly points. Rohit was one of the honourable exceptions in a disappointing season, stacking up 404 runs at an average of 36.72 and a strike-rate of 147.98 from 13 matches, showcasing his six-hitting skills with 19 sixes from 273 deliveries faced.

The Steady March Slows Down

Rohit was now a regular in the Indian white-ball squads, but batting largely between numbers four and seven, he didn't have a great time of it. His unquestioned skills meant he would get a long rope, but he was starting to test the patience of the selectors and the team management. Rahul Dravid's decision to step down as captain ahead of the 2007 season and Dhoni's inspirational leadership skills in South Africa had catapulted the Jharkhandi to the captaincy of both limited-overs set-ups, and Rohit was fortunate that both Dhoni and Gary Kirsten, who had taken over as the head coach by now, continued to invest in his talent and potential.

Between his ODI debut in Belfast in June 2007 and the home series against South Africa in March 2010, Rohit averaged a modest 25.62 across 42 matches; he had only four half-centuries in 39 innings, numbers that did his immense talents no justice. Dinesh Lad is convinced that those poor returns had much to do with Rohit moving house to Bandra at the end of the tri-series in Australia.

'He wanted to stay in Bandra because he could be closer to the BKC ground, which was a fair call in a way, but I was insistent that he must not make the move,' Lal says. 'I opposed his decision because I felt the atmosphere in Bandra wouldn't be great. He was still practising with me but I felt shifting to Bandra could be a diversion because there are so many distractions in an area like Bandra. In a way, the sequence of low scores wasn't a huge surprise. He didn't devote as much time to cricket as he used to and as he should have. He had also got a lot of money from the IPL and perhaps that also played a part.'

Strangely enough, while Rohit was struggling to cope with the demands of international cricket, his first-class record remained stunning over three consecutive seasons, between 2008–09 and 2010–11. He followed up an aggregate of 881 runs (average 80.09) in 2008–09 with 718 (avg. 79.77) and 768 (avg. 96) in the two subsequent seasons, hammering seven hundreds including a career-best unbeaten 309 against Gujarat in the Ranji Trophy in December 2009. At this rate, a Test call-up was surely imminent, never mind that he was yet to crack the limited-overs code completely.

Red Ball Call-up

Rohit had briefly lost his place in the ODI XI after the West Indies tour of July 2009, at the conclusion of the T20 World Cup in England. He played no part in the tri-series in Bangladesh in January 2010, where India lost the final to Sri Lanka, even though he was in the squad. Like two and a half years before, while Bangladesh brought him huge disappointment, it also gave him the chance to break into the Test side after two separate mishaps involving two of India's all-time greats.

During the first Test in Chattogram, V.V.S. Laxman split the webbing between his right thumb and forefinger while fielding in the slips during the Bangladesh second innings—an injury that would keep him out of cricket for a month or so. As if that wasn't bad enough, Dravid was struck on the side of his face by a bouncer from Shahadat Hossain in India's first innings in the next Test in Dhaka, which started on January 24. Dravid, who had made a hundred in the first Test too, was batting on 111 when the ball didn't get up as much as he had expected it to and sustained a fractured jawbone which would obviously take some time to heal. But time wasn't India's ally. The first of two Tests against South Africa was to begin in Nagpur on February 6 and neither Laxman nor Dravid—who would miss the entire series—was available for selection. Although the team management and Laxman himself held out hope of a timely and miraculous recovery, it didn't come to pass.

Thus, Rohit found himself in the extended Test squad alongside the uncapped duo of S. Badrinath, the prolific right-hander from Tamil Nadu, and Wriddhiman Saha, who was drafted as the second wicketkeeper behind Dhoni and ahead of Dinesh Karthik, who had donned that role in Bangladesh. With Yuvraj Singh also unavailable due to a wrist injury, Badrinath and Rohit were primed to replace Dravid and Laxman—huge shoes to fill, but nevertheless an exciting opportunity against a high-class South African pace attack manned by the unmatched Dale Steyn, Morne Morkel, Wayne Parnell and Jacques Kallis.

In December 2009, with their commanding 2-0 conquest of Sri Lanka at home, India had climbed to the No. 1 Test ranking for the first time and they cemented their hold on the top-dog status with their 2-0 sweep of Bangladesh. But they had to avoid defeat against South Africa if they hoped to extend their stay at the top of the ladder. Since their readmission to international cricket in 1991, few teams had acquitted themselves with greater credit in Tests in India than the Proteas. After a 1-2 loss in 1996, South Africa regrouped to deliver a stunning 2-0 coup in the two-match series in 2000. It took a seven-wicket haul from Harbhajan in the second innings of the second Test in Kolkata in 2004 for India to edge that showdown 1-0. In 2008, India had to wage a grim battle to bounce back from an innings defeat in the second Test in Ahmedabad to win the final game in Kanpur and square the three-match series 1-1.

To say, therefore, that the hosts had their work cut out against a redoubtable outfit under Graeme Smith, an experienced hand at the rudder, would be stating the obvious. Without Dravid and Laxman, India were shortchanged even before the first ball had been bowled. But in Badrinath and Rohit, they had two names for the future coming off loads of runs in domestic first-class action.

A Steady Climb, and Huge Setbacks

Rohit was named the captain of the Board President's XI in a two-day game against the South Africans in Nagpur, which ended just three days before the start of the Nagpur Test at the new VCA Stadium in Jamtha. Batting at number four, skipper Rohit made 20 before falling to left-arm paceman Parnell, while Pujara, at number six, was dismissed for 17 by off-spinner Johan Botha. The following day, Rohit linked up with the Indian Test squad while Pujara returned to domestic duty. Despite the best efforts of the medical team, Laxman's injury didn't heal in time, and Badrinath and Rohit were informed the day before that they would be making their Test debuts.

For both, it was a massive moment. Badrinath was 29, having made his Ranji Trophy debut for Tamil Nadu nine seasons back and stacked up runs galore. When he eventually called time on his career in 2016, he had amassed more than 10,000 first-class runs at an average of 54.49, helped along by 32 hundreds in 145 matches. Rohit, by contrast, was only 22 but he was a merited selection who had worked his way up the ranks in just three and a half years. The duo spent a restive night, excited at what lay ahead because at the time—perhaps even now, though one can't be absolutely certain—to win a Test cap was every cricketer's ultimate dream.

Fate, though, has a funny way of dealing with hopes and ambitions. Manoj Tiwary's injury had brought Rohit into the white-ball spectrum internationally, and injuries to Dravid, Laxman and Yuvraj facilitated his early entry into the Test squad. Having smiled benevolently on him, the cricketing gods threw the young man a curveball just minutes before Dhoni and Smith walked out for the toss. During a pre-match warm-up routine, Rohit twisted his ankle while playing football and saw his Test aspirations go up in smoke. It wasn't a serious injury—he would be back in action just a week later, on February 14—but it was enough to prevent him from playing his first Test.

'It was a terrible blow,' admits Laxman, 'and he was obviously sad, but he was not someone who was overthinking it. He was sad because he was certain to play the Test, to make his debut, and then something like this happened. But he was not distraught—he didn't think as if it was the end of the world. You could make out that he was disappointed, but he wasn't brooding over it for the entire duration of the game, moaning about it or asking, "Why me?" I found that very appealing. After a session or so, he was back to his normal self; his calmness and equanimity stood out even then.'

By the time of the second Test, which India had to win after Steyn had sent the team tumbling to an innings loss with seven wickets in the second innings in Nagpur, Laxman was available for selection and Badrinath had done his cause no harm with a 56 in the first innings on debut. Rohit was back to the grind of domestic cricket, unaware that it would be three and a half more years before he would become a Test cricketer.

ODI Comeback

Within three weeks of the Nagpur injury, Rohit returned to the ODI XI after more than seven months on the sidelines, racking up 48 against the South Africans in the final game in Ahmedabad, which Sachin Tendulkar sat out. In just the previous game in Gwalior, the little master had become the first male batter to register a double-hundred in a 50-over international. Tendulkar was rested for the inconsequential final game—India had already taken a winning 2-0 lead—and Rohit, batting at number four, put on 95 with Virat Kohli for the third wicket. India slumped to a heavy defeat after allowing South Africa to post 365, and while no one knew at the time, that wasn't to be the first time Kohli and Rohit would be engaged in a meaningful partnership at the highest level.

After a break for the IPL, where Deccan Chargers failed to defend the title won in 2009 in South Africa, India returned with a disappointing run at the T20 World Cup in the Caribbean. Immediately after that, they went on a limited-overs tour of Zimbabwe in May 2010. They were to take on the hosts and Sri Lanka in a triangular tournament, followed by a T20 series against Zimbabwe. Given how quickly it followed the T20 World Cup, India rested several senior players and Suresh Raina was entrusted with the captaincy of a relatively inexperienced side. India failed to make it to the final of the three-nation event, but it was a memorable competition for Rohit.

Nearly three years after his debut, Rohit had his first international encounter with three figures at the beautiful Queen's Sports Club ground in Bulawayo. In the opening game on 28 May, he made a fluent 114 against Zimbabwe, hitting six fours and four sixes in his 119-ball knock. Batters crave a century for various reasons—for some, it is the ultimate reiteration that they belong in international cricket, while for others, it means a little more breathing space and the prospect of more games on the trot to prove their worth. The quest for hundreds has been a constant since the inception of the game and while it is unfair to judge the value of batters on the number of centuries alone, there is a certain inimitable contentment in getting to that coveted landmark.

Rohit's first international ton had taken a while coming, though he couldn't entirely savour it because it came in a losing cause. But enjoying the high of a hundred can be an addiction, so it was no surprise that two days later, in the same ground, Rohit breezed to a second century, this time hauling his team over the line against Sri Lanka. A cracking square-cut against Ajantha Mendis, his sixth four, took him past 100 off as many deliveries, and Rohit was unbeaten on 101 when skipper Raina brought up the winning run. If there was pure joy when he reached the Promised Land for the first time, there was added cause for celebration this time because he had stayed on till the end and taken the team past the finish line. With two hundreds in three days, Rohit's confidence was at an all-time high. The 50-over World Cup, in India, Bangladesh and Sri Lanka, was eight and a half months away and Rohit couldn't have laid down the marker any more emphatically.

Overlooked: Reality Check and Introspection

However, what ought to have been the springboard to a place in the World Cup squad turned out to be a false dawn as Rohit's returns plummeted dramatically thereafter. He had just one half-century over his next 16 ODI innings and effectively played himself out of World Cup contention with scores of

11, 9, 23, 1 and 5 in the five-match series in South Africa in January 2011, India's final engagement before the World Cup. To no one's surprise, Rohit wasn't picked for the big bash, with Yusuf Pathan winning the nod following a more impressive lead-up to the competition.

'2011 was a memorable one for all of us. I remember watching it from home, every single match, every single ball which was being bowled and that was being played,' Rohit told the International Cricket Council in 2023, during the Trophy tour before the 50-over World Cup in India. 'There were two kinds of emotions—one was, obviously I was not a part of it, so I was a little disappointed. I decided I was not going to watch the World Cup, but again, the second memory I remember was that India was playing so well, quarterfinals onwards—you know, the big quarterfinal against Australia. It was a brilliant finish by Yuvi (Yuvraj Singh) and Raina at the end. And then the semifinal was against Pakistan. I know how the pressure is on all these players when playing these games. I can only imagine the pressure that each player must have gone through at that time.'

Rohit was gutted when the squad was announced and his frustration mounted with each passing game and victory as India carved their way through the draw, eventually besting Sri Lanka in the final at Rohit's second home—Mumbai's Wankhede Stadium. Being left out of the World Cup party was a second body blow to the young man in 12 months and predictably, he called up Lad to complain and crib, perhaps hoping for a sympathetic ear and a virtual comforting arm around his shoulder.

Instead, Rohit was given a reality check by his coach.

'I asked him to reflect on his performances in the several months leading up to the World Cup,' Lad recalls. 'I told him that he had got a lot of opportunities but had done nothing with those chances. I asked him how he could have been selected with the returns he had in his last 16 innings (290 runs at an average of 18.13). He was tried out in different positions—at all slots from number one to seven, except for number six—during that phase because I think the team management desperately wanted him to succeed, but he just couldn't score runs. I told him that there was no point having oodles of talent if he didn't devote time to the game.'

Stunned by his coach's reaction, Rohit embraced introspection and acknowledged the older man's wisdom. 'He promised me that he would practise so much and with such intensity that I would have no cause for complaint. And that's exactly what he did,' Lad's pride in his prized pupil shines through. 'He was at the BKC (Bandra-Kurla Complex) every day, from 7 a.m. to 5 p.m., sweating it out, determined to put the disappointment of not being selected for the World Cup behind him and keen to start all over again. After that, he has seldom disappointed.'

That was when Abhishek Nayar, friend, teammate, roommate, confidant, and eventually one of the assistant coaches with the Indian senior side, got into the act. He left no stone unturned in his bid to get his mate up to scratch. '2011 was something that changed the way he thought about fitness,' Nayar reveals. 'What has changed is the way he prepares, the way he looks after his body. I stayed with him at his Bandra house, we slogged it out for six to eight hours a day. In six weeks, he lost seven kilos. He was fitter, leaner, meaner. Rohit has never looked back ever since.'

By then, Yuvraj Singh and Rohit were not just close buddies but also Bandra neighbours. 'In the months before the World Cup, they made Rohit bat at all numbers. He even opened in South Africa just before the World Cup when Sachin got injured,' Yuvraj recounts. 'If he had got a consistent run in the middle order, a settled slot, I'm sure he would have got the nod. But anyways, after the team was announced, he came to my home. We had new team jerseys for the World Cup and he said, "These jerseys are so cool. I'm feeling very bad that I am not going to see myself in them." That really affected me.

'I told him, "Shaana (that's what I call him), let's go for dinner." At dinner, I told him that he had to work harder than before to come back into the team. I told him that if the India jersey was that important to him, he had to earn it. With the talent he had, there was no reason why he couldn't play for the country for the next ten years consistently—remember, at that point, he was in and out of the team. He channelized all his energies towards getting better, getting fitter, and look where it has taken him today.'

4

The Birth of the White-ball Opener

When India won the ODI World Cup for the first time in England, in 1983, it was against all odds. Few gave them a ghost of a chance to make it even to the semifinals, and several members of Kapil Dev's squad viewed the last of the 60-over World Cups as a pit stop on their way to a series of exhibition matches in the United States. It was no surprise—given that their only win in six previous World Cup games, spread over two editions, had come against a motley bunch playing as East Africa—that the bookmakers had given them 66-1 odds of going all the way.

But inspired by their captain's words and deeds, and riding on the plethora of all-rounders well suited to exploit assistance from the conditions, India stunned the cricketing world with their 43-run conquest of West Indies at Lord's on 25 June that inexorably altered the balance of power in the sport.

Rejoining the World Champions

By 2011, India were no longer outsiders. Instead, they began the competition as overwhelming favourites to double their tally of ODI World Cup titles. The weight of expectations was humongous but India had the wherewithal, cricket-wise and temperamentally, to set them aside and make their way through the draw. They weren't dominant, forced to dig deep at various stages, playing out a tie against England in Bengaluru, and suffering an extraordinary meltdown against South Africa in Nagpur when they slumped to their only defeat.

But come the knockouts and they were a side on a mission—brushing aside holders Australia, arch-rivals Pakistan and 1996 champions Sri Lanka in the quarters, semis and final, respectively, to regain their status as world champions. It was inevitable—given that the victory had come in front of their adoring home fans—that the stocks of the side and the players concerned would grow massively.

In normal course, to break back into a World Cup-winning ODI team would have been difficult for Rohit—and anyone else, for that matter—if not almost impossible. But with a couple of senior batters opting for a break during the tour to the West Indies that came immediately on the back of IPL Season 4, which started a week after the conquest of Sri Lanka on 2 April at the Wankhede Stadium, Rohit was thrown another lifeline.

Determined not to look a gift horse in the mouth and channeling his inner steel, Rohit had a fabulous tour of the Caribbean, with three half-centuries in five innings whilst

The Rise of the Hitman

batting at number five. He followed it up with three more fifties, on the trot, against West Indies at home later in 2011 and seemed to have cemented his place in the middle order. But in those days, everything didn't always work out to plan when it came to Rohit Sharma.

A stunning loss of form, starting with the tri-series in Australia in February 2012, translated to a solitary half-century and eight single-digit scores in 13 innings, in four countries—Australia, Bangladesh, Sri Lanka and at home. With scores of 5, 0, 0, 4, 4 and 4, Rohit played himself out of the XI for the home series against England in January 2013.

By then, Sachin Tendulkar had bid adieu to the ODI format. His forty-ninth ODI ton—a record that lasted until the 2023 World Cup when Virat Kohli went past the little master—in the Asia Cup encounter against Bangladesh in Mirpur in March 2012, took him to a 100 international centuries. He played just one more match after that, in the same tournament, against Pakistan. But it wasn't until later in the year—ahead of the three-match series at home against the same opponents—that he officially announced his retirement, creating a huge vacuum at the top.

Tendulkar had been an almost exclusive opener in ODIs ever since his accidental elevation to the top in New Zealand in 1994, and while India did have other resources—not least Virender Sehwag and Gautam Gambhir—the need for a long-term partner for the latter was heavily felt by Dhoni and Duncan Fletcher, the erstwhile head coach. To that end, Ajinkya Rahane was tried out as an opener, and—once Sehwag was left out midway through the series against Pakistan—was brought

The Birth of the White-ball Opener

back to partner with Gambhir at the start of the five-match faceoff against England.

The Englishmen had returned for the ODI series after a Christmas break, on a high after defeating India in a Test series in the latter's home-turf for the first time since 1984-85, and brought that form to the first ODI in Rajkot which they won by nine runs. Rahane weighed in with 47, but efforts of 4 and 0 in Kochi and Ranchi, respectively—in games that India won—meant that the experiment with him at the top of the order was wobbly. As an opener, Rahane had just two half-centuries in his first 16 ODIs.

In a last throw of the dice, when the teams moved to Mohali for the fourth game, with India holding a 2-1 advantage, Rahane was replaced at the top by Rohit. He had previously opened the batting thrice in South Africa in January 2011, making just 29 runs.

This time would be different.

Decisive. Game-changing. Career-altering.

It was a regular wintry January Wednesday, and yet it wasn't. It was 23 January 2013, a huge date in Indian, indeed world, cricket—though no one knew it at the time.

Opening in ODIs

Dhoni chose to field first—intending to open up a winning 3-1 lead—and India did well, keeping England down to 257 for seven on a good batting surface and a smallish outfield. It was up to the strong batting order to get the job done, which was a wonderful mix of youth and experience. And then there was Rohit, in a position he wasn't entirely familiar with internationally but grateful merely to have worked his way back into the mix after a brief period on the sidelines.

Up against him and Gambhir were Steven Finn, Tim Bresnan and Jade Dernbach—admittedly not the most intimidating trio of pacers—and spinners Samit Patel, James Tredwell and Joe Root. It wasn't quite now or never, but it was getting dangerously close to that point.

Rohit responded to the new challenge in brilliant fashion. From the first ball, it was clear that he was in his element—the strokes flowed freely and the nerves, if any, were kept beautifully hidden. His languid grace was on full view at the PCA Stadium during half-century stands with Kohli and Suresh Raina. By the time he was trapped in front by Finn, he had breezed to 83 off 93, setting up the five-wicket win that Raina finished off with aplomb. Rohit the white-ball opener had arrived. There would be no turning back.

India's next assignment was the Champions Trophy in England in June 2013, a tournament they had never won outright. By now, a new opening pair was in place—Rohit and Shikhar Dhawan. It was a pair that would serve Indian cricket fabulously well for the next half-dozen years as they took down bowlers of all variety in all conditions with practised ease.

The Sharma-Shikhar Duo

'As a white-ball player, everybody now knows what Rohit has achieved,' says R. Sridhar, the former India fielding coach.

'Even in my early days with the Indian team—from the third quarter of 2014—he was somebody who worked very hard on his game. With Shikhar, he formed a very formidable opening pair. They were the perfect foil for each other. They knew each other very well, they were good friends on and off the field. And that left-right combination catalyzed a golden phase for India in ODI cricket and T20 cricket; they rubbed off very well on each other.'

Over 115 innings as an opening combination, Rohit and Dhawan added 5,148 runs at an average of 45.55, with 18 century stands and 15 more in excess of 50, and are ranked fourth in overall ODI history, behind Sachin Tendulkar-Sourav Ganguly, Adam Gilchrist-Matthew Hayden and Gordon Greenidge-Desmond Haynes.

'They were special not just in ICC tournaments but also in other games mainly due to the deep understanding of each other's games. Another feature of their opening success was their chemistry on and off the field,' continues Sridhar. 'They were just chalk and cheese in terms of personalities, but Rohit loved Shikhar for his flamboyance and for his openness and Shikhar thrived within the brilliance of Rohit. Their batting styles too complemented each other.

'Rohit was known for his patient, calculated approach and then taking on the *Vishwaroopam*. He balanced out Shikhar's more aggressive attacking style at the top of the order. They built so many match-winning partnerships for India that you can't even keep track of them, it was unbelievable. Such was their understanding that when one was stuck, the other took over. When one was going slow, the other upped the ante.

In my time with the Indian team, in those seven years, I can't even start to tell you how many times they won matches and set up situations.'

The contrasts, Sridhar believes, are what made them a great hit. 'Shikhar was always great fun on and off the field. He was genuinely open—he is the "what you see is what you get" kind of a person; Rohit always calmed him down and he was the perfect ally for him. Rohit and Shikhar—I won't say the best opening pair for India because we had Sachin and Sourav; in the era before them, Sachin and Sourav were brilliant in ODI cricket. But I think Rohit and Shikhar come a very, very close second to them, especially in the 2015 and 2019 World Cups when they were absolutely magnificent.'

Double Hundreds

Nearly three and a half years after the second of his successive ODI hundreds in Zimbabwe, Rohit added a third hundred in October 2013, against Australia in Jaipur. It was beautifully brutal—on a flat surface, the Aussies had amassed 359 for five but India hunted that target down with ridiculous ease. When the winning runs were scored, there were 39 deliveries and nine wickets in the bag. Rohit and Dhawan put on 176, Kohli came and finished things off in a rush by making a 52-ball 100 not out during a second-wicket stand of 186 with Rohit. When the end came, Rohit was unbeaten on 141 off just 123 deliveries. By now, he was marrying aggression with consistency; much like his idol before him, it had taken Rohit nearly a half-dozen years to surge to the top of the One-Day batting order.

The Birth of the White-ball Opener

But once he reached the summit, it was a different ballgame altogether.

As it turned out, Jaipur was merely the appetizer. The main course came a fortnight later at the M. Chinnaswamy Stadium in Bengaluru. The seven-match series was tied at 2-2—there were two no-results—when the teams squared up for the decider. There was everything to play for in a series totally dominated by the bat, where the bowlers had merely been serfs brought in to dole out freebies on the flattest, most unforgiving of surfaces. Rohit was at his subliminal best, treating the Australian attack—for want of a better word—with absolute *disdain*. Boundaries flowed off his bat with unerring regularity, the sixes comfortably outnumbering the fours. In all, there were 12 fours and 16 sixes. As the spectators got their money's worth, Rohit joined Tendulkar and Sehwag in the 200-club with a magnificent 209 off 158 deliveries. Notwithstanding the benign nature of the track, it was a wondrous compilation marked by great timing and placement. The ball went exactly where he wanted it to, his command total and complete.

'To me, that first double-century in One-Day cricket was the turning point,' observes W.V. Raman, former Indian opener and head coach of India Women, and acknowledged as one of the country's best cricket analysts. 'I think that's when he realized that there are things that he could do as long as he didn't hesitate. Of course, he became very meticulous with the passage of time in terms of what he needed to do as a batter. But that knock made him realize the things that he needed to do without being in no-man's land mentally.

'What he's done tremendously well is that he has not thought too much about what he needs to do. He has decided (to) let things pan out organically. Initially, he was a bit hesitant whether to play his shots or not. Once he's taken the route of opening, his desire to play shots, his desire that "I'm going to really boss over the bowling," that's been noticeable. There's no question of the hesitation factor coming into play. And once he's done that, it's worked wonders for him. Whatever he's done—be it being aggressive—he's done it in the same fashion without compromising on his basic quality, which is being easy on the eye. He's never made batting look a laborious exercise. That is what is his speciality, just like it was V.V.S. Laxman's.'

In One-Day matches, Rohit's approach in the early part of his opening stint was very simple and unfussy. He was a master at reading the conditions, of course, but he was also forever looking to dominate the bowling. He had the technique to bide his time, give the early periods to the bowlers if the ball did a bit, secure in the knowledge that he had the game to catch up even if he took his time early on. That mindset was to change, especially when he became the captain, but for nearly a decade after he became a regular white-ball opener, his consistency was staggering for someone who played as many shots as he did.

Sridhar had a ringside view of the Rohit magic for seven years in his capacity as the fielding coach of the national team between 2014 and 2021. 'The first time I met him at the National Cricket Academy was very, very brief,' Sridhar recalls. 'We didn't know each other very well then but later on, when I went into the Indian team, that's when I got to know him so much better.'

The Birth of the White-ball Opener

Sridhar came on board with B. Arun and Vikram Rathour—as part of team director Ravi Shastri's entourage—midway through India's tour of England in 2014, just before the start of the white-ball leg. 'The first match in Bristol got rained off and it was in the second ODI in Cardiff that I first saw Rohit in action from the dressing-room. He batted really well (52 in India's 304 for six) but he broke the middle finger of his right hand while attempting to take a catch and missed the remaining part of the series.'

For someone who was enjoying his time at the top of the tree and instilling dread in bowlers around the world, it was an untimely injury—by now, Rohit was getting used to this—but he went back and nursed that injury while continuing to work on other aspects of his cricket. He wasn't back in action until November 2014, but when he did return, he announced his arrival in the most emphatic fashion, with 264 in his very first game against Sri Lanka at Kolkata's Eden Gardens.

'It's been a decade now, but that continues to remain the highest individual score in ODIs,' Sridhar points out. 'It was a fabulous innings, which is stating the obvious. That was when the whole world saw the enormous ability and the exceptional talent that Rohit possessed. Of course, he had already made a double by then, but this showed that the sky was the limit, that he wasn't someone who was easily satisfied. The 264 at the Eden showed what Rohit was all about—he is mega, he is big, he is someone who you can expect to set his eyes on big things and then do everything in his control to go out and achieve that. From then on, as I got to know him better, my admiration for him grew exponentially.

The Rise of the Hitman

'I really appreciated his hard work—for all the skills bestowed upon him, he is someone who worked very, very, very, very hard. As a batter, he knew exactly what his game was. He understood his strengths, his areas of limitations, and always played accordingly. He studied the opposition bowlers very meticulously, he left nothing to chance. I don't need to say it, but his runs didn't come about by accident, his success wasn't without great effort even if he makes batting look so effortless.'

Within two years of being thrust into the role of the opener in white-ball cricket, Rohit had made that slot his own on the back of a string of exceptional efforts. The runs flowed freely and unchecked, with style and grace, and at a frenetic rate. He wasn't just a short-span destroyer either, as testified by the knocks of 141 not out, 209 and 264, within a span of 13 months. These would become commonplace in time to come. India's supporters had feared for life after Tendulkar in 50-over cricket. Those fears were comprehensively laid to rest by another Mumbaikar who has done the legend proud not just with the quantum of runs, but also in the manner in which he has eked them out all over the world, against all bowlers and in all competitions, be it bilateral series or prestigious global tournaments.

5
White-ball Legend

Rohit's white-ball career is clearly a tale of two halves—before 2013, when he batted in the middle order but struggled to express himself, and after 2013, when he was pushed to open for the country in both variants on a permanent basis and took to it like to the manner born.

The middle-order position didn't allow Rohit to bat with the freedom he coveted. A strong batting line-up meant he didn't always have as many deliveries to showcase his devastating stroke-play as he would have liked. While he has blossomed into an exceptional six-hitter, a trait that was apparent even during his early days, the middle order seemed to shackle his creativity.

The Hitman

Then came Mahendra Singh Dhoni's masterstroke at the start of 2013, which led to the birth of the 'Hitman', as the world knows him today. Dhoni was a great believer in Rohit's ability and realized, some might say a little late, that both he and the team would benefit from the right-hander being given first bite at the cherry, so to say. The opening slots were hardly up for grabs until then, it must be remembered. When Rohit broke through, Sachin Tendulkar, Virender Sehwag and Gautam Gambhir were all firmly entrenched, and it was impossible to look beyond them. By the beginning of 2013, though, Tendulkar had retired, and the two Delhi batters were on the downswing.

Dhoni's immense faith in Rohit's capabilities, the logjam in the middle order, his own travails while walking into an older ball and the gaping holes at the top of the batting tree, all combined to catapult Rohit to the opener's status. It wasn't quite the last throw of the dice as might have been six years later, when he was promoted as Test opener, but going out to bat against a brand new ball, with field restrictions in place, worked out beautifully for him and his team, just as Dhoni's impeccable intuition had predicted.

The runs flowed by the bushel—attractive, dominating, muscular runs, without a hint of power or crudity. Rohit gracefully rode on the back of his excellent basics, exploiting the new freedom accorded to him, and erected one striking edifice after another.

'Rohit is someone who hits through the line against the fast bowlers,' V.V.S. Laxman observes, deconstructing the white-ball behemoth. 'When he was going in at number five or number six, he wouldn't get that opportunity (to hit through the line) because the ball was already old and the field well spread. But when he became an opener—a great decision by M.S., I must say, and (coach Duncan) Fletcher—he was able to play his natural game and he was getting value for his shots, because he was always a boundary and six-hitter. He was not someone who believed a lot in singles.

'His first instinct was always a six or a four. And if that didn't happen, okay, he looked for singles. But even his singles were not so much with soft hands but always hitting the pockets, with full-fledged drives or backfoot cuts. His intention and instinct were always to hit a six or a four.'

Warming to the theme, Laxman continues, 'With the field restrictions, he was able to get that space, the ball coming on to the bat. As a batter, he enjoyed the ball coming on to the bat and that's why I was not surprised he got lots of runs in Australia in the tri-series in 2008 even though he was batting in the middle order. With personal experience, I can say that those are the pitches where he would flourish because the ball would come on nicely and he just had to time the ball. Once he started to open, the pace on the ball helped him. He was able to get hundreds. I believe that is something which happened with Sachin also. When you are batting at number four, five and six, even in One-Day cricket, how many hundreds can you get? But as an opener, Sachin started getting hundreds and so did Rohit after him.

'And then, Rohit started getting double hundreds. That's because of the nature of his game, the ability to hit good balls for sixes, and the fact that he knew he had that ability. He also had the confidence that he was playing proper cricketing shots and that by following his natural instinct of being aggressive and a boundary hitter, he could actually put a lot of pressure on the opposition bowlers.'

The Rise of the Hitman

While Rohit thrived on pace on the ball, it was his preparation and improvement against spin that truly impressed Laxman. 'His game against the spinners really improved drastically,' he opines. 'You can see that from the areas in which he started scoring as his career progressed. It was not only from extra-cover to mid-wicket. As his career blossomed, he was able to access the square pockets on both sides. Like, he was going late and playing the cut shot through the point region, and then he started to sweep. He can play the slog sweep, he can play the normal conventional sweep, and in the last two years or so, he has started playing the reverse sweep also. That shows that he was always looking for ways to score quickly, to put the bowler under pressure, to call the shots, to let everyone know who the boss was.'

Once his first hundred—as an ODI opener—came against Australia in October 2013, the floodgates well and truly opened. Rohit was now secure in the knowledge that he was no longer an experimental opener—the slot was his for keeps. That triggered an astonishing run of consistency as he and Dhawan gave India the starts that Virat Kohli and the others could build on. Kohli rightly went on to be recognized as the ultimate 'chase master', but much of it had to do with the platforms laid by Rohit and Dhawan, who had that uncanny understanding that doesn't come easily.

The first of Rohit's double hundreds came less than a year after he opened the batting, also against the Aussies, in Bengaluru in November 2013. It was a breathtaking exhibition of the magical mayhem Rohit could unleash. His 209 that evening might have been the first of his double tons but everyone knew for certain that it wouldn't be his last.

Not by a long shot.

Lazy or Lucky? Or Both?

It took Rohit a little over a year to double his tally of double centuries. He had gone 15 innings without an ODI century and missed several games due to injuries. But no one believed that he had *lost* it. Those 15 hundred-less knocks had produced four half-centuries and just when he was beginning to hit his straps in England in August 2014, he had to fly back home with a broken finger, hours after making 52 in Cardiff.

The three months away from international cricket left him ravenous and Sri Lanka paid the penalty on his comeback, at the Eden Gardens in Kolkata. It was at this theatre of dreams that, in November 2013, Rohit had celebrated his belated Test debut with a sparkling 177. A year and one week later, he clattered the gargantuan 264, unloading all his pent-up frustrations on the hapless islanders.

During this period, India were focusing on building towards the 2015 50-over World Cup in Australia and New Zealand, and Rohit was an unstoppable force in the longer limited-overs format. By now, scoring hundreds had become second nature for him. But he wasn't content with scoring small centuries. The epochal 264 was backed up by 138, 137 and 150 in the next 12 months, by which time he had raced to his maiden T20I hundred as well, against South Africa in Dharamshala in October 2015.

'Rohit was one who was always easy on the eye and the

reason for that was that he had a minimum of movement before the ball was delivered, something that you would always find in the touch players,' W.V. Raman, himself one of India's foremost touch players, notes. 'They don't make too many trigger movements, as they call it, before the ball is released. That's one of the reasons why he gave everybody the impression that he had a lot of time to play.

'Over a period of time, he's realized that he's better off doing what he can do best, which is to stay still for as long as possible and then try and work things out as the innings progress. He was guilty of perhaps chasing at deliveries a bit too far away from him earlier on in his career. That's because when your technique is not complicated, there is a tendency for you to think you can reach out to anything or you also like that feeling of the ball coming and hitting your bat. So, you tend to reach out only with hands sometimes when you don't have to play because you would see that happen with a lot of touch players.

'Sometimes, they even get the foot across because they're not restricted either in terms of their bat speed, bat flow, or the extent to which they can get their foot going either sideways or down the track. That is one of the things which made Rohit the batter he was and he is. And that's also one of the reasons why he was getting out, reaching out to deliveries and people thought that, you know, he was a bit casual, he was a bit lazy, earlier on in his career.'

Lazy is a tag attached to most cricketers who make batting look easy and effortless. Sometimes it is used as a euphemism for lucky, as if to suggest that they have been bestowed with a gift by a higher power, which they haven't worked hard enough to deserve. Often, there is a touch of envy when the term lazy is bandied about regarding batsmanship. Such as, 'Why can't I bat like that?' Clearly, Raman could, so you understand where he is coming from.

'They (the critics) would talk about the talent he had and how he was not making use of that talent. But what he's done well is not to pay heed to the negative comments that were made of him,' Raman adds, perhaps drawing from his own experiences in his early years in the sport. Long before he became an analyst and a coach, Raman was an extraordinary left-hand batter who moved up from the tail-end of the batting order to the very top, where he treated the best of bowlers as if he were playing a bunch of schoolkids in a chilled-out, Sunday-afternoon outing. 'He stuck to the conviction that his technique was good; all he had to do then was to try and be better in terms of when he started playing his shots.

'Once he sussed that out, he started doing well. He found his feet in international cricket. He learnt the knack of getting runs and there's been no stopping him. Obviously, his talent was too much for him to not get runs in international cricket. V.V.S. Laxman is who I always tend to think of when I see Rohit bat, because both of them had that felicity of playing both spin and pace without any fuss or without giving you the impression that they were hurried when they played the quickest bowlers. And in Rohit's case, he had to obviously adapt to various things, not only the formats but also the positions.'

In his early days as international white-ball opener, Rohit wasn't quite the destructive beast that he has become since

The Rise of the Hitman

assuming the Indian captaincy. He did make the most of the field restrictions but didn't take his chances like he does now, playing the percentages and trusting his game enough to understand that his ball-striking would allow him to catch up with the run rate even if he began somewhat cautiously in deference to the conditions. His acknowledged six-hitting skills, identified even at a nascent stage by Laxman and Raman, among others, meant he couldn't be kept quiet for long periods. The short ball held no fear because he was a consummate puller, an offshoot of the cement-pitch practice under Dinesh Lad, and his wonderful timing and nimble feet enabled him to dominate spinners once he had got his eye in. Perhaps the only Achilles' heel was the ball coming in against the angle from the left-arm over pace bowler, though it wasn't a big enough issue to prevent him from scoring runs anywhere in the world, against any kind of attack.

From being just one of the players within the set-up, in less than two years of becoming an opener Rohit had become one of India's most influential performers in both 50-over and T20 cricket. Almost every Indian victory had a Rohit touch to it; Kohli made himself the ultimate when it came to chasing down totals—his role embellished by his propensity to stay till the end and get the job done—but in his own understated and entertaining manner, Rohit made himself indispensable with muscular contributions to numerous winning causes. From averaging in the early 20s and striking at less than 78 per hundred balls faced in his first 86 ODIs, during which he only struck 23 sixes, Rohit flourished at the top of the tree. By the end of the ODI series in Sri Lanka in August 2024, he averaged nearly 57 in 50-over internationals; in 176 innings, he had hammered 308 sixes, lending credence to his well-founded 'good-ball-six-hitter' reputation.

Hitman was an automatic and natural moniker given the ease with which he hunted down oppositions and took the bowlers to the cleaners. Even as his 50-over stock grew, Rohit didn't allow the grass to grow under his feet in the T20 format. It might appear straightforward, expecting those flourishing in the longer limited-overs version to replicate the magic in the shorter one, but as K.L. Rahul bears testimony, that isn't necessarily the case. Apart from the fact that the same colour of ball is used in both variants, there's not much similarity between the two. Rohit made the seamless adjustment from one format to the other, the long haul in 50 overs swapped for shorter, more bruising efforts in the 20-over shootouts.

To score one century in a T20 International is no mean feat; to have five of them, eight and a quarter years apart, is little short of outstanding. For a little over five years since making an unbeaten 111 against West Indies in November 2018—his second unbeaten T20I century in three innings at the time—Rohit didn't flirt with the three-figure mark until his 121 against Afghanistan in Bengaluru in January 2024. If his sustained remarkable consistency didn't yield the coveted milestone, it was only because of a shift in mindset. In the past, where he used to milk the bowling after a breakneck start, he now kept batting at one gear—the topmost he could unearth. Team totals were on a dramatic upsurge—greater familiarity with the format and universal flatbeds triggering a massive increase in the scoring rate. Determined to ensure that

The Rise of the Hitman

India didn't get left behind, especially once he assumed the all-format captaincy in early 2022, Rohit took it upon himself to set the tone, thereby commanding a similar attitude from his teammates.

'It's not about the individuals, it's not about the hundreds,' Ajit Agarkar agrees. 'He's the guy who's got three double-hundreds in ODIs, five hundreds in T20I. But now he's not batting for runs as such. As the Selection Committee (Chairman), as a leadership group, it makes our task very easy. Basically, you're just following what you're trying to tell people. You're setting an example. I always felt the captain should be one of your top players, if not *the* top player. It just makes it easier for him to command that respect and demand things of people because you're going out there and performing.

'But to play the way he did in both the 50-over and 20-over World Cups in 2023 and 2024 respectively... It's one thing to have that intent or have that thought to do it. But to actually go out and do it against some of the best attacks in the world, wow!' Agarkar says, admiringly. 'Then you're telling the rest of your team—this is how we are going to play, I'm going to start it.

'Of course, you have to have the ability also to do so, which he has in abundance. It's very easy to say that we want to play in a particular way. But if the captain starts doing it, he sets the right example. People have no choice but to follow. That's why it becomes easier for everyone concerned in a team sport.'

6

The IPL Kingpin

It was when Mahendra Singh Dhoni's team was creating history in South Africa at the inaugural T20 World Cup in September 2007 that the Indian Premier League was formally launched, with franchises to be based in eight top cities. The team auctions were held on 24 January 2008 and the first-ever player auctions on 20 February 2008, when the Indian team was playing in a triangular series in Australia with Sri Lanka as the third team.

From Mumbai to Hyderabad: The Inaugural Indian Premier League Season

After the team auctions, five 'icon players' were identified, who would be the face of the franchises based in their city. For Mumbai Indians, it was Sachin Tendulkar. Rahul Dravid was Royal Challengers Bangalore's marquee player, Sourav Ganguly was for Kolkata Knight Riders, Virender Sehwag for Delhi Daredevils, and Yuvraj Singh for Kings XI Punjab. Chennai Super Kings and Rajasthan Royals didn't boast anyone from the respective states/cities deserving of the icon status. That left Deccan Chargers, for whom V.V.S. Laxman was the designated icon.

As the rules stood, the icon player would get 15 per cent more than the most expensive player of the team procured at the auction. Laxman voluntarily surrendered his icon status so that his team owners could utilize the additional amount at the auction and augment the cricketing activities run under the aegis of the Hyderabad Cricket Association. It was a typical Laxman move, made without fuss or without attracting the same blaring headlines that would have followed had Tendulkar or Ganguly ceded their icon status.

Even if he was not the icon, Laxman was the captain of the franchise and one of the first names in his bucket list at the auction was Rohit. Deccan Chargers left no stone unturned in their effort to acquire Rohit's services, shelling out US $750,000 for the 20-year-old who, at the time of the auction, was not even eight months young in international cricket.

Laxman's first sighting of Rohit had come during the three-day final of the KSCA MRF Trophy in August 2005, when his team, Indian Airlines, took on the National Cricket Academy, led by Ambati Rayudu and coached by Venkatesh Prasad. Rohit batted for a little over an hour and a quarter on the first morning—making a fluent 45—but that was enough to make a lasting impression on the gifted Hyderabadi.

'The first impression was that he was someone who had a lot of time playing the fast bowlers—he had a fraction of a second more,' Laxman recalls. 'He had this front-in-front trigger movement and he was playing a lot of balls on the rise. Against the spinners, I felt he was not able to play as fluently as he was against the fast bowlers. He had not yet developed that game against the spinners where he could hit boundaries or easily rotate strike. That was understandable, because when someone has spent a lot of time playing against fast bowling and when the ball suddenly is coming slowly, he was still adjusting his timing to the slow delivery, to the flighted delivery.

'But then when I next saw him at the T20 World Cup (in 2007)—and thereafter (in) the tri-series in Australia (2008)—the progression was very rapid. Just two years previously I had seen him as an Under-19 boy, and now he was playing against the likes of Brett Lee at his peak, and he was playing with a lot of ease, playing some beautiful-looking shots. But what I really liked was that his game against the spinners had developed. Straightaway, you knew that the guy had the mindset to want to improve, the ability to learn quickly. Even though I hardly knew him, he made quite a first impression on me.'

It was on the back of that impression that Laxman urged the Deccan Chargers management to plump for Rohit at the auction. 'He was one of our important players going into the auction,' he agrees. 'We wanted him because he had the ability, because he was a special talent. There was something different about him; anyone who's got that fraction of a second more time is always going to be exceptional. He was a gifted player, abundantly talented.'

Rohit didn't disappoint Laxman or the leadership group within the team even though Deccan Chargers brought up the foot of the table in the inaugural edition of the IPL. His off-spin was utilized very sparingly—he only bowled four overs in the entire tournament—but he stood out with the bat, amassing 404 runs in 13 matches. His average (36.72) and strike-rate (147.98) were excellent, given that he was often ploughing a lone furrow in the middle order, which added further lustre to his four half-centuries. Rohit's first tryst with the IPL was an unqualified individual success; over time, he would fuse that with team triumphs too, including five as captain with Mumbai Indians.

'What I loved about him is that in every match he took a lot of responsibility,' Laxman goes on. 'He was just starting his international career but the way he played was like someone with a lot of experience. He had the ability to hit not only the spinners, but also the fast bowlers by planting himself on the front foot and clearing the infield or even the boundary by playing proper cricketing shots, which he continues to do. A majority of his strokes were in the V, from long-on to long-off, and he could hit sixes at will against the fast bowlers. Furthermore, most of the time when he walked out to bat, there was pressure on the team. He had a very good IPL season—many of the shots he played were a delight to watch. Many of the senior players in our side (Adam Gilchrist, Herschelle Gibbs, Shahid Afridi among them) felt that this guy had talent. We agreed that we would be disappointed if he didn't play a hundred Test matches.

'From that younger generation in our squad, he naturally became a leader just through the confidence he was exhibiting, along with his flamboyance. We didn't have a great season, but he was contributing—not only with the bat, but also in the team meetings. He was vocal with his views, he was a leader of the youngsters, whether it was R.P. Singh or Pragyan Ojha. By the second season, he was already regarded as a senior member of the team whose views would be taken very seriously.'

Under the Spotlight

For any sportsperson at the highest level, it is the second season that is the most crucial. In the first season, the individual is a bit of an unknown commodity. But, especially if they court success, a lot of analysis is conducted by the time the next season comes around and they often become marked by various oppositions. Rohit was also somewhat afflicted by the second-season blues in the IPL, his returns marginally falling to 362 runs (average 27.84, strike-rate a modest 114.92) when the tournament moved to South Africa in 2009.

The pitches weren't at their best, considering that the tournament was staged in April–May, which isn't South Africa's cricket season, and that played a role in his diminished returns. But Rohit also pulled his weight with the ball, finishing with 11 wickets, including a stunning best of four for six against Mumbai Indians, ironically, which also included a hat-trick. His economy was an excellent seven runs per over as his off-spin was used judiciously. While it was his captain, Gilchrist, who was declared the Player of the Tournament, Rohit's role in Deccan Chargers' title run was immense.

'Along with having the talent, he was a thinking cricketer even at that stage,' Laxman avers. 'Whenever people used to say that he's only talented but he's not a performer, it would rankle me because he was very hardworking and he *was* performing, but maybe not to the standards others expected of him all the time. Not once did I see him taking shortcuts as far as practice sessions were concerned. He was a natural fielder; he used to move swiftly on the ground, he also took a hat-trick. In those three years with DC, I saw how hard he worked on his game, how he left no stone unturned in his bid to be the best version of himself.'

A third good season with the bat in 2010 meant that teams were lining up for Rohit's services. The mega auction ahead of IPL 2011 was the stage where a fierce bidding war unfolded, at the end of which Mumbai Indians emerged triumphant, shelling out US$2 million to herald Rohit's homecoming. It was a spectacular coup with the local lad teaming up with the franchise based in his city, a huge cause for celebration given how hot a property Rohit had become. No one knew at the time, of course, that that would be a seminal moment in the history of not only the franchise but also Indian and world cricket.

A New Homecoming

Rohit walked into a Mumbai Indians dugout with acknowledged superstars of the game—the legendary Tendulkar, who was the captain, Sri Lankan giants Sanath Jayasuriya and Lasith Malinga, Harbhajan Singh, who would go on to lead the team in 2012, experienced Kiwi James Franklin, and a sensational emerging talent in Kieron Pollard. In his three years with Deccan Chargers, Rohit had shown that he wouldn't be overawed by the big names. Teamed with the biggest name in Indian cricket, he continued to be his own man, treating the big boys with respect but not deference.

In his first season with MI, Rohit topped 350 runs for the fourth edition in succession, slotting nicely into the middle order. His franchise went down to Royal Challengers Bangalore in Qualifier 2, but the general consensus was that Rohit's first season with his new home was a worthwhile one, if not an unqualified success.

Under Harbhajan in 2012—Tendulkar had ceded his captaincy—Mumbai Indians made it to the Eliminators again, but surrendered to Dhoni's Chennai Super Kings this time. Rohit amassed his highest tally of runs yet, at 433, embellished by his maiden T20 century. He had celebrated his twenty-fifth birthday during the tournament and was about to step into his sixth year as an international cricketer. Within 12 months, he would embrace a responsibility that would define him.

Ahead of IPL 2013, Mumbai Indians roped in Anil Kumble as the team's mentor to complement head coach John Wright and his support staff. Harbhajan asked to be relieved of the captaincy and Dinesh Karthik was briefly looked at as a possible replacement. When that didn't work out, Mumbai Indians became determined to ensnare former Australian captain Ricky Ponting as their new skipper.

Ponting didn't have a great deal of experience playing T20 matches, let alone leading a team in the format, but MI needed a steadying hand at the helm of affairs. 'There was a bit of apprehension when the suggestion of Ricky as captain was made to the owners at that time because Ricky had come to the end of his international career,' Kumble remembers.

The Rise of the Hitman

'More importantly, as a T20 player, it was not easy for someone right towards the back end of his career to come in. But before the auction, when John and I sat down and analyzed the team, we felt that all it needed was somebody who's been there and done that in big moments. Ricky's won World Cups, he's been a part of teams that consistently won in big tournaments and he's a big-match player. We felt that was the only thing that was possibly missing in the squad.'

Mumbai Indians won three of their first four games but then lost two in a row, the second of those defeats being a nine-wicket hammering by Delhi Daredevils. As if that wasn't bad enough, Ponting had hit a serious trough; in five innings, he made only 52 runs, his strike-rate an embarrassing 69.33. 'Ricky's performances weren't anything to write home about,' Kumble says, 'and it's not easy to go to someone and say you need to step aside. But to his credit, Ricky realized that he wasn't pulling his weight and stepped aside on his own, which was big of him.'

Rohit Sharma, Captain

Once that happened, Rohit became an automatic choice to succeed the Australian. Three days after the battering at the hands of Delhi Daredevils, Mumbai Indians were scheduled to play Kolkata Knight Riders at the Eden Gardens. 'When John and I went to his room in Kolkata and sat him down and told him he was ready (to be the captain), he didn't even bat an eyelid,' an admiring Kumble reveals. 'That gives you the confidence—you know you are sort of taking a chance, but you also know that at least this guy is not hesitating. He was very clear when he led the team that he was in control. You could see that he was not overawed by the big names in the team and in the dugout.

'Of course, Ricky was good with the team too. It's a natural thing these days when somebody who is an international captain is not the captain of his franchise; it's a part and parcel of T20 cricket now. But that wasn't necessarily the case more than a decade back. We got back to winning ways in Rohit's first game as captain and subsequently we started winning more matches. Once you get the wins under your belt, the confidence grows. Rohit was very assured as the tournament progressed and come the Champions League, we didn't even have to think of leadership. We had already won the (IPL) trophy; Rohit managed it really well, he managed all the bowlers superbly. Captaincy is about managing your bowlers, not the batting line-up. It's about strategy when you're on the field and he looked pretty assured. In even intense moments, he looked in control. Of course, he had (Lasith) Malinga, Harbhajan, Mitchell Johnson, all these guys, but you still have to manage the resources and in some of the low-scoring games, he was brilliant in controlling the game. That tells you that you know what you're doing. So that way, he was very assured.'

One of the things that struck Kumble about Rohit in their early interactions as mentor and captain, respectively, was how expressive the latter was. 'I didn't associate that with Rohit,' Kumble concedes. 'When I first met Rohit, I didn't think he would be that expressive in team meetings. But he would come across and talk about tactics, and all that came

The Rise of the Hitman

naturally to him when he was captain. That was refreshing to see; he was in total control. With each year, with every passing match, he became even more confident. It was a pleasant surprise in terms of him being expressive in a group because I at least had not interacted with the Rohit where he would be the first one to speak. But in this group, he was the leader, and he immediately took ownership of the leadership role and started to build a narrative of what he wanted to have in the team in terms of culture, in terms of how he wants the players to respond to situations. He also had the respect of everyone else in the team because everyone knew his capabilities as a player, as a match-winner.'

It's a view shared by Laxman. 'When I say that he became a leader in 2008 itself, it was due to his nature where, irrespective of whether he was performing or not, his behaviour off the field would be very, very normal,' Laxman notes. 'And that's never ever changed, especially with his peers. I think him becoming the Mumbai Indians captain was the best thing that happened to Rohit and, in the long run, to Indian cricket. That changed everything. He had to lead by example. What happens is that if someone is very naturally gifted, preparing well and trying his best to perform but not able to string together consistency for some reason, there might be a temptation to play for yourself. But when he became the MI captain, he no longer thought about his position in the team. He no longer thought, "I have to perform to be in the playing XI." In my view, his thought process maybe shifted from scoring his own runs to how he can win a match for his team. That's the best shift for any player, because invariably then you are playing more important innings and consistently at that. And that shift with Rohit happened while playing for Mumbai Indians.'

Leading an IPL team is so completely different from leading an international side. Even before leading a team, the first challenge is to procure the right personnel—fill the gaps, plug the holes. Then comes the trickier part, especially with regard to international players, of letting them know that despite their track record, price tags and value in country vs. country contests, the dynamics of IPL don't allow for their inclusion in the playing XI. That was perhaps the most demanding task in the early days of the tournament, telling the big-ticket overseas stars that they had to warm the bench. But people-management is something that has come naturally to Rohit and therefore he could convey even difficult messages with grace and composure, his openness and honesty endearing him to even the recipients of unwelcome news.

'A lot of it also came down to the respect he commanded in the dressing room,' points out Parthiv Patel, the former India stumper who played under Rohit at MI between 2015 and 2017, when the franchise won two titles. 'Everybody knew that whatever decision he took was only in the interest of the team. There were no personal biases. And on top of everything, he was very good with his communication. He'd tell you why you're not playing. That's where Rohit was fantastic. To me, communication is very, very important—when the honesty comes out, you get the trust of the players. And that's what Rohit got—the trust of every player.'

The cares and responsibilities of captaincy didn't adversely impact Rohit the batter. His appearances at the bowling crease became more and more sporadic—indeed, he didn't bowl a single delivery for six consecutive editions, between 2015 and 2020—but his bat continued to run hot. In his first half-season as captain in 2013, Rohit made 538 runs—the only time he has topped the 500-run mark in his IPL career. Two years later, when Mumbai won their second crown in 2015, his runs were marginally less, but his strike-rate had grown to 144.74 (from 131.54). And even though Rohit had started to open in both white-ball formats for India, the mentor at his franchise wanted him in a different role. 'I was still sort of aligning him to play in the middle order for Mumbai Indians, which was not really what he wanted; he wanted to open the batting,' Kumble says. 'But I felt it was the best for the team that he bats in the middle order.' In a mutually happy and productive compromise, Rohit largely batted at number three in the 2015 campaign, including in the final where he smashed a 26-ball 50 against Chennai Super Kings after coming out to bat in the first over following Parthiv's dismissal.

Having been one of the foot soldiers during Deccan Chargers' title run in South Africa in 2009, Rohit masterminded five title runs in eight years as the Mumbai Indians' general. Alongside Dhoni, he holds the record for the most titles as IPL captain; like Dhoni, he has also now overseen an electric T20 World Cup campaign, with an unbeaten run through the tournament to boot. Parthiv comes up with a Dhoni parallel of his own. 'There was one similarity with Dhoni as a captain, in terms of how Dhoni gave a lot of space to players in his early days as skipper, though he changed over time and started telling people what to do,' Parthiv observes. 'But with Rohit, it's always about giving every player that space, telling them that they had reached that level purely on the back of their merits and therefore he didn't have to micromanage them. That's where he was very good in the dressing room.

'Rohit was well prepared as a captain. On the ground, people talk about his spontaneous decision-making but he spent a lot of time with analysts. In that sense, he was different from Dhoni—Dhoni would not watch videos, but Rohit was the central figure in watching videos, spending a lot of time with bowlers, all of that. He could make captaincy look very easy mainly because of his preparation.

'And more than being a fun guy, he was very relaxed. He was never tense—there was no tense energy around the dressing room. When Rohit spoke, he would make you believe that the toughest thing in the world wasn't that tough at all. That was best illustrated during the 2017 IPL final.'

In that final, Rohit chose to bat but Mumbai Indians were restricted to 129 for eight by Steve Smith's Rising Pune Supergiant in Hyderabad. 'No one gave us a chance at all of defending that small score,' Parthiv reminisces. 'But Rohit just wanted to keep pushing the game deep, ensuring that no one slackened, keeping energy levels up, almost visualizing how the turnaround would happen. And just that made a lot of us believe. After a while, everyone in the field was convinced we could defend 129, there was so much self-belief. To communicate the toughest thing in the simplest way, that is Rohit's principal USP.'

For the record, Rohit's MI pulled off a heist, securing victory by one run after Washington Sundar was run out trying to level the scores. 'He was always ready to listen to suggestions,'

Parthiv points out. 'There were times where he would actually ask for suggestions. As a keeper, he had given me that free hand to set fields—he'd tell me that the angles were my territory; that he was not going to get into that. He was very good at sharing responsibility because—especially in 20-over cricket—everything can't be only the captain's job.'

Rohit might now be lost to Twenty20 International cricket as both batter and captain following his retirement after the World Cup success, but his influence on the game at that level will resonate for a long time to come. Of course, the IPL is still his oyster, though some might say that he is rapidly bringing a touch of T20 batting to his approach as a Test opener too.

7

The World Cup Behemoth

To be overlooked for the 2011 50-over World Cup at home was a massive blow for Rohit. That disappointment mounted as India were crowned champions on 2 April at the Wankhede Stadium in Rohit's hometown of Mumbai. Once he got over that omission, Rohit chose to use it as a springboard to greater things instead of moaning and cribbing about how he had been hard done by.

'He was disappointed, yes,' observes Abhishek Nayar, Rohit's long-time friend and Mumbai teammate, 'but it was more anger and, you know, "Come on, let's show them, let me get fitter, let me work harder."' Armed with fierce determination, Rohit managed to work his way up the batting order to the opening slot by January 2013.

Vikram Rathour, India's batting coach between 2019 and 2024, was part of the national selection panel from 2012 to 2016, which would eventually trigger the rise of Rohit as a prodigious white-ball opener. 'He was always a special player and so everybody wanted him to play, at whatever number,' recalls Rathour. 'Basically, the decision of him opening came from the team management. And, as selectors, we completely backed it; we agreed that we should try this.

'Once he started opening, he had a phenomenal time. It just changed everything, there was no looking back. And what I feel is that eventually, even though it was more than six and a half years later, that was what created the pressure for him to open in Test matches as well.'

ODI World Cup Debut

Rohit had to wait until 15 February 2015, more than seven and a half years after his One-Day International debut, to play his first 50-over World Cup game. Fittingly enough, it was a marquee contest, against Pakistan at the Adelaide Oval. India hadn't lost to Pakistan in five World Cup head-to-heads until then, starting from Sydney in 1992. It was essential that they keep the 100 per cent record going, and that Rohit and his equally attacking opening partner, the left-handed Shikhar Dhawan, set the tone.

In preparation for the World Cup, India had been involved in a triangular series against the host nation and England. Their opening outing had been against Australia at the MCG where Rohit made a typically brilliant 138, accounting for more than half of India's tally of 267 for eight. Only Suresh Raina of the rest topped 20 and India paid the penalty for a tepid batting display with Aaron Finch playing the lead role in Australia's comfortable four-wicket victory. But it wasn't so much the result that worried the Indians.

The World Cup Behemoth

Rohit picked up an unfortunate hamstring injury during that knock that ended his interest in the tri-series. India failed to make it to the final as their World Cup preparations took a massive hit. But, as dispiriting as that was, the bigger concern was around Rohit and whether he would recover in time to take his place in the playing XI against Pakistan.

Fortunately, Rohit's rehab went according to plan and he took his appointed place at the top of the order beside Dhawan. But it wasn't quite a debut to remember. One of the criticisms of Rohit at that stage was shot-selection, be it in Tests or the limited-overs formats, and his dismissal to a premeditated pull against Sohail Khan, the right-arm quick, when the ball wasn't short enough for the stroke, attracted due criticism. Rohit's contribution to an opening stand of 34 was a 20-ball 15, but with half-centuries from Dhawan and Raina bookending a measured 107 from Virat Kohli, India amassed 300 for seven and ended up trooping home as comfortable victors by 76 runs.

His tournament went from bad to worse a week later at the MCG when he was dismissed for nought, run out at the bowler's end after having set out looking for a non-existent single and being sent back by Dhawan. As he trudged off, distraught, he must have thought what more he needed to do to make his World Cup appearances count. After all, by then, he already had made two ODI double-tons to go with numerous centuries.

When would his World Cup jinx end?

'One of the things that really struck me at that time, and even later when Rohit wasn't quite doing justice to his ability in Test cricket, is that we all were saying, "Oh, why is he not performing? Why is he not performing?" You know, nobody ever said it's time for him to be replaced. Nobody felt that, which is very strange in India, isn't it?' W.V. Raman wonders. 'Because we are very quick to discard people. But Rohit touched a chord in people even before he became the giant he is today. It was just a case of the breakout happening. Not even the biggest of his detractors said it was time for him to be replaced.'

The World Cup Take-off

Rohit's World Cup career finally took off against UAE on a bouncy WACA strip in Perth that facilitated his stirring backfoot play even though he didn't have too much pace to work with. An unbeaten 57 set him up for the tournament ahead and he backed it up with 64 against Ireland in Hamilton but truly sprung to life in the quarterfinals against Bangladesh at the MCG, the venue of his last international century two months ago.

Bangladesh had pulled off a huge coup by putting England out of the tournament and making it to the knockout phase; England were to recalibrate their approach to the white-ball game following their humiliating first-round exit and go on to sing the redemption song four years later when they won the World Cup on home soil for the first time. But once they were sent packing, and it became clear that Bangladesh would be India's opponents in the last-eight stage, a majority felt India's presence in the semifinals was but a mere formality.

Until that point, Rohit had played only five ODIs against Bangladesh, with the modest total of 73 runs and a highest of 26. He did approach the 19 March quarterfinal with two half-centuries in his last four knocks in the World Cup, but he hadn't quite made the kind of impression he would have liked. Rohit couldn't have chosen a more appropriate occasion to make his first World Cup hundred—in his first knockout game—though it wasn't without controversy.

Rohit had no direct role in the drama that unfolded at the MCG, apart from being the batter at the time. He had made his way to a sedate 90 off 101 deliveries when he tonked a full toss from Rubel Hossain down the throat of deep mid-wicket. Even as the Bangladeshis celebrated his 'fall' at a vital stage of the game—with the death overs approaching and India seeking to bat them out of the game—on-field umpires Aleem Dar and Ian Gould ruled that the delivery was illegitimate because the full toss was above the waist. Subsequent replays suggested otherwise, but the decision stood and Rohit went on to keep his tryst with three-figures, eventually falling for a superb 137 off 126 deliveries.

It was largely due to his effort that India amassed 302 for six and pulled off a comfortable 109-run victory, but the aftershocks of the no-ball that wasn't continued to reverberate, primarily in Bangladesh. Mustafa Kamal, the Bangladeshi who was the president of the International Cricket Council (ICC), told national television channels, 'There was no quality in the umpiring. It looked like they took the field after it (the outcome) was pre-arranged.'

His comments drew strong reactions from Dave Richardson,

the former South African wicketkeeper who was then the ICC Chief Executive. 'The ICC has noted Mr Mustafa Kamal's comments, which are very unfortunate but made in his personal capacity,' Richardson said, not mincing words. 'As an ICC President, he should have been more considerate in his criticism of ICC match officials, whose integrity cannot be questioned.

'The no-ball decision was a 50-50 call. The spirit of the game dictates that the umpire's decision is final and must be respected. Any suggestion that the match officials had "an agenda" or did anything other than perform to the best of their ability are baseless and are refuted in the strongest possible terms.'

India-Bangladesh cricketing relations were already strained even though the rivalry was one of unequals and despite Bangladesh achieving Test status in 2000 almost entirely thanks to Jagmohan Dalmiya's efforts. Over time, there would be an added needle to the India-Bangladesh contests with the latter coming close on numerous occasions to toppling Big Brother only to falter with the finish line in sight.

Rohit had no control over the controversy of the catch, though that did take some sheen off his excellent effort. After a long wait to prove himself on the biggest stage of all, Rohit had finally made his statement, but some of it was lost in the din surrounding the no-ball and the charges and counter-charges that flew in the face of it.

India's reward for their defeat of Bangladesh was a tilt at Australia in the semis. In a one-sided contest, Australia triumphed by 95 runs on their way to an unprecedented fifth title, Rohit signing off his maiden World Cup with 34. In his first World Cup, he finished as the fifteenth highest run-getter—India's second highest behind Dhawan (412). His 330 runs had come at an average of 47.14 and a strike-rate of 91.66—more than passable, but hardly electrifying. In many ways it mirrored India's campaign, which was like the proverbial curate's egg—only good in parts.

2019 World Cup: Individual High, Collective Low

By the time the next edition came around in England in 2019, Rohit had come to be acknowledged as one of the all-time white-ball greats. He had become the only man to stack up three double-centuries and had 17 ODI hundreds to his name. He was in tremendous form going into the tournament, topped off by successive fifties at home against Australia in India's final two matches before the World Cup. Alongside Dhawan and Kohli, he formed a formidable top-three that carried all of India's hopes.

Indeed, so prolific had this trio been in the months before the World Cup that India didn't pay much attention to the pivotal number four spot. Going into the tournament, that position didn't appear very important because the top three seldom failed to deliver, and therefore, didn't give the following batters many opportunities to showcase their wares or ease into their positions. Consequently, they were a little unprepared for the carnage that unfolded in the semifinal against New Zealand in Manchester when a target of 240 proved beyond them.

For the first time since 1991–92, when Australia and

New Zealand co-hosted the event, the 50-over World Cup reverted to an all-play-all ten-team round-robin format, with the top four making it through to the knockout semifinals. The fact that, theoretically, all teams would get to play nine matches apiece was insurance against the fickle English weather which queered the pitch in the middle part of the tournament. Mercifully, it held true for most of the second half.

India faced a tricky start to their campaign. There are no easy games in the World Cup, it goes without saying, but India's first three opponents were South Africa, Australia and New Zealand. If they got on a roll, India would have one foot in the semis after just the first week; if they faltered, the road to the semis would be full of potholes and towering obstacles.

A tacky deck greeted the teams when South Africa and India arrived at Southampton's Rose Bowl for the latter's first encounter. By then, South Africa had played, and lost, their first two matches, both at The Oval in London. The first was the tournament-opener against the host nation which England won by 104 runs. The second was an even more shattering defeat, by 21 runs, to Bangladesh in a tall-scoring contest. South Africa were desperate to get on the board, which perhaps explained Faf du Plessis's decision to bat first because both defeats had come whilst chasing.

Leg-spinner Yuzvendra Chahal was the middle-overs star after Jasprit Bumrah struck twice in his first spell as India kept South Africa down to 227 for nine. Numerically, the target wasn't huge, but India had to bat well—*very* well—against a strong bowling unit which included pacers Kagiso Rabada and Chris Morris, and wrist-spinners Imran Tahir and Tabraiz Shamsi.

India made sedate progress despite losing Dhawan in the sixth over. Run-scoring was laborious even for the usually fluent Rohit and skipper Kohli. India were never in any real danger, but they also didn't boss the run-chase. Rohit quickly cottoned on to the fact that he had to anchor the innings—that new batters would find the going tough—so he set his natural attacking instincts aside and ground out a commendable century, his second in three World Cup outings. When Hardik Pandya thwarted any artificial excitement by hauling India home with six wickets and 15 deliveries to spare—the comfortable margin belied the tenseness of the chase—Rohit was unbeaten on 122 off 144 deliveries, showcasing his determination to conquer his inner demons and to bat according to the needs of the team and situation.

'That discipline as an opener was very much needed for someone like Rohit,' says Laxman. 'I just wanted to see whether he could do that or not. But he has proved it. That also shows his mental strength. That's one of the reasons why he got five 100s in the 2019 World Cup; the hundred he got against South Africa was the best because on that wicket, and against that quality bowling attack—it was spongy and the other batters actually struggled—Rohit got almost a Test match-like century. That's the change he brought to his batting, it was purely because of his mind.

'He didn't worry too much about his technique, the technique didn't change. The feet position remained the same and it has remained the same. The way he uses his hands is still the same. But it's just that his control over his instincts, his control over his mind, and having that clarity as far as his batting plan is concerned—that was beautiful to watch, just beautiful to watch.'

With South Africa out of the way, India next travelled to the English capital to take on the Aussies, the defending champions, at The Oval. Four years is a long time in international sport and both teams had played plenty of ODIs against each other in that intervening period. But it was inevitable that the mind would occasionally travel back to the Sydney misadventure. This time, India batted first on a terrific deck and Rohit and Dhawan got down to business straightaway, adding 127 at 5.5 per over, before Rohit fell for a 70-ball 57. Dhawan blazed to a hundred, Kohli hammered 82 off 77, and India's 352 for five was 36 too many for Australia.

Two for two was a grand start!

The euphoria of another clinical performance was offset by the loss of Dhawan for the rest of the tournament after sustaining a fracture to his left thumb when he was struck by a short ball from Pat Cummins. 'The two had established a great partnership when Shikhar got hit. He broke his finger, and he wanted to come in (retire hurt),' R. Sridhar observes. 'He was in seething pain but Rohit urged him to stay on and fight it out. He said, "If you go in and if you remove the glove, there is no way you'd be able to bat in this tournament again. This is your chance, you bat through pain. This is a very important phase for India, we have to win this game."

'He urged Shikhar to keep batting, and Shikhar kept batting. He listened to Rohit. He kept batting and scored that magnificent hundred, but he could not play in that World Cup again.'

The World Cup Behemoth

Dhawan's non-availability was a potentially game-changing development; India had gotten used to blazing starts from Rohit and Dhawan, but now the former would have a new opening partner in K.L. Rahul. The Karnataka batter was no stranger to opening the innings or batting alongside Rohit, but it was still a rapid adjustment in the middle of the tournament that created a hole in the middle-order.

After a no-show against New Zealand in rainy Nottingham, India ran into familiar foes Pakistan in the scheduled fourth outing at Manchester's Old Trafford. By now, the teams were reduced to playing each other only in continental and global competitions. Therefore, every showdown became that much more magnified. In a stunning display of stroke-making, Rohit put the vaunted Pakistani pace attack in its place, aware that the wonderful batting strip demanded a big score on the board for the bowlers to defend. Rahul was an admiring silent partner in an opening salvo of 136 as Rohit got on the bike and sped away, reaching his 100 off just 85 deliveries. It showed his innate cricketing sense and the ability to bat differently on different surfaces against different oppositions.

A fourth ODI double-ton seemed to be on the cards as Rohit clattered to 140 in the thirty-ninth over, when a cheeky scoop resulted in a catch to short fine-leg. Rohit was furious with himself but he had done plenty damage by then. India's 336 for five was enough for them to continue their winning streak against Pakistan in World Cups, this time by a margin of 89 runs on the DLS Method.

With two centuries and a fifty in three innings, Rohit was positively buzzing when he was brought down to earth by

The Rise of the Hitman

twin failures—1 and 18 against Afghanistan and West Indies, respectively. India managed to edge the former in a thriller and crush the latter with a powerhouse bowling display, which meant that when they ran into England in Birmingham, they were well on top of the table with five wins (and a no-result) from six games.

Edgbaston was a collective disappointment with the match degenerating into a farce towards the end and Mahendra Singh Dhoni making only a token assault in a near-impossible chase, but Rohit returned to century-making ways with 102 off 109—just the kind of start India needed after England amassed 337 for seven. The defeat by 31 runs was a temporary blip; Rohit and Rahul put on 180 against Bangladesh and 189 against Sri Lanka in their last two matches. Rohit was the first to be dismissed each time. Against Bangladesh, his 92-ball 104 took him level with Kumar Sangakkara for the most hundreds in a single World Cup (four). This time there were no dramas or controversies; no no-balls to throw a spanner in the works.

'He was not fit against Bangladesh, he had a small hammy (hamstring) issue by the time we played against Bangladesh, because he had scored so many runs and run so many singles and doubles and threes, not just for him, but for everyone else,' reveals Sridhar. 'He was fitter then than what he is now, but the physical exertions were catching up. But still, he scored a very, very sublime hundred to ensure the game was a piece of cake for India.'

His 94-ball 103 against the Sri Lankans catapulted him to rarefied World Cup territory; Rohit had five hundreds in just eight innings at the World Cup—an extraordinary accomplishment that showcased his versatility, hunger, drive and fitness.

'He had enormous self-belief right from the start of the tournament,' observes Dinesh Karthik, who also played in that World Cup. 'There was (an) insane amount of detached attachment as well, where he was very much attached but was able to put things in perspective. At that stage, he had his daughter (on tour) who was just recently born, so he obviously had a very positive distraction off the field. He was very calm in his demeanour throughout the tournament. His ability to consistently—at the back of the mind—have India at the forefront in terms of winning games was phenomenal.'

Carrying a hat-trick of centuries into the semifinal against New Zealand, Rohit was undone by the skilful Matt Henry on the reserve day. India began needing 240 in 50 overs to make their second final in three editions. Using the overcast skies to his advantage, Henry got one to straighten after shaping in—the two previous deliveries had kept coming in with the angle—and caught Rohit's outside edge, the ball nestling in Tom Latham's gloves. Rohit's second-over dismissal for one was a setback India failed to recover from, stumbling to 24 for four and 92 for six, then mounting a stirring fightback through Ravindra Jadeja but falling 18 short in what turned out to be Dhoni's last international fixture.

'Rohit had a phenomenal tournament,' Sridhar remarks. 'His ability to anchor the innings while maintaining a high strike-rate, it was something else. He was relaxed off the field. He took care of the team's energy, kept it nice and high. He put on a masterclass in how to play in a big tournament. Elegance, timing, aggression, composure, technical brilliance, reading the game, reading the pitch, pacing the innings, flawless shot-selection—these are the things that set him apart from other batters in that tournament. He played like a dream, he dominated bowling attacks. He had a serene demeanour at the crease. And everyone knows how he bats—every run he scores is easy on the eye, every run he makes is a good-looking run. It made for great viewership. That tournament pretty much defined Rohit as an opening batsman and set up the rest of his career.'

Rohit finished as the tournament's leading scorer with 648 runs—one more than David Warner—averaging 81 and scoring at 98.33 runs per 100 balls faced. These numbers deserved better than a second semifinal exit, but Rohit was the first to put his hand up for not making his form count in the semifinals. 'He had a standout tournament, but even after getting nearly 650 runs he was far from happy,' Karthik reveals. 'After the semifinal loss, he said, "I don't care about the runs, the hundreds. We lost the semis, so all these runs don't mean as much to me as it would have if I didn't score at all and we ended up winning the World Cup." That has always been his kind of attitude—he is a very team-driven man.'

To score as many runs and hundreds as Rohit did in the space of five weeks is no mean feat. The play-travel-play routine is a demanding one, especially in a tournament as intense as a World Cup. Each match day was followed by a bus journey to the next venue, and the time for preparation and recovery was minimal. Rohit's commitment to the cause was most obvious to Basu Shanker, who was the Strength and Conditioning Coach of the team at the World Cup.

'He didn't miss a single gym session,' Basu notes. 'The day after the match was a recovery day and we had gym sessions and then practice. Throughout the World Cup, he was in the zone. He had this tunnel vision. He took care of his body definitely better than he had in the previous years.'

Basu was with the Indian team for four years from 2015, and the longer he was with the side, the more fitness-driven he saw Rohit become. 'I will never forget this,' he whispers. 'Towards my last one year, he once told me, "If I ever slacken, just call me and tell me." That way, he was very easy to handle. If I went up to him and said he was doing something wrong, he would listen. He simply had no ego. He embraced the modernization of fitness along with Virat. And he also made sure that whatever was instructed, he always followed it. His fitness routine was very specific and he followed it to a tee.'

A two-time World Cupper now, with six centuries across the two editions, Rohit had drawn abreast of the great Sachin Tendulkar for the most hundreds in the tournament's history. Tendulkar's six tons came in 44 innings, Rohit got to that number in just 17. And he wasn't finished yet. Two semifinal losses weren't quite on his menu, but when he left Manchester in July 2019, shattered after the New Zealand heartbreak, he didn't know that four years on, he would mastermind another assault in the World Cup—this time not just as the battering ram opener but also as the captain who would lead by example, who would walk his talk all the way.

8

Opening Gambit

Test Debut

Rohit's much delayed Test debut was the stuff of dreams. Having waited more than three and a half years—since twisting his ankle moments before his first scheduled appearance against South Africa in Nagpur in February 2010—he celebrated the occasion with a magnificent 177, batting at number six against West Indies in Kolkata in November 2013. It was an innings of extraordinary grace and maturity after he walked in at a critical moment, at 82 for four in reply to the Caribbeans' modest 234 all out. There was a certain poignancy to the fact that his arrival at the batting crease was thanks to the dismissal of his hero who was playing his final Test series, the peerless Sachin Tendulkar.

India soon slumped to 83 for five, when Virat Kohli fell, and were staring at a potential deficit when Rohit was joined by his captain, Mahendra Singh Dhoni. The latter steadied the ship with the debutant through a stand of 73, after which Rohit ramped things up in R. Ashwin's company. The two graceful right-handers put on 280 for the seventh wicket when Rohit eventually was trapped leg before by Veerasammy Permaul, the left-arm spinner. As he walked off to a standing ovation after six hours of entertainment that yielded 23 fours and a six, one sensed that this was just the first of several Rohit specials.

That feeling was reinforced in the very next game—Tendulkar's farewell Test—at the Wankhede Stadium in Mumbai, Rohit's home ground. Again batting at number six, but walking into a solid platform, Rohit bashed 111 of the 180 runs scored when he was at the crease, adding 80 with last man Mohammed Shami to finish unbeaten with 11 fours and three sixes from a mere 127 deliveries. Where he had embraced careful circumspection at the Eden, Rohit was a free spirit at the Wankhede, showcasing his versatility and adaptability in the longer format.

With centuries in his first two Tests, Rohit joined Mohammad Azharuddin and Sourav Ganguly in an illustrious list. It was taken for granted that these two efforts were just the beginning—that Rohit was the real deal who was here to stay, that he would be the bulwark of the Indian middle order alongside Cheteshwar Pujara and Kohli in the post Dravid-Tendulkar-Laxman-Ganguly era.

Injuries and Comeback(s)

However, things took an unexpected turn. Rohit suffered an extraordinary slump thereafter, scoring just four half-centuries in his next 30 Test innings. Injuries didn't help his cause either. Just when he was beginning to find his feet back in Test cricket on another of his comebacks in August 2016, after eight months in the wilderness, he suffered a thigh injury during an ODI against New Zealand in Visakhapatnam. This, after having made 238 runs in five innings in the preceding Test series when he averaged 79.33.

Anil Kumble was in his first series as head coach when Rohit returned to the Test XI in August 2016 in the Caribbean, making 9 and 41 in Gros Islet in the only Test where he batted. 'He only batted in four Tests when I was the coach, that thigh injury was very untimely because he was in the middle of a fine run,' Kumble observes. 'He scored 80-odd (82) and won us the Kolkata game against New Zealand. It was a green-top, the ball was swinging and seaming all over the place and he was brilliant in the second innings. He also made an unbeaten half-century in the next Test in Indore, but then the injury put him out of action for more than a year in Test cricket.'

By the time Rohit returned to Test cricket in November 2017 against Sri Lanka in Nagpur, Ravi Shastri had taken over as head coach. Like on debut, Rohit produced a subliminal century against the Lankans and followed it up with twin half-centuries in the drawn Delhi Test. In five Tests, spread across 15 months, he had made one hundred and five fifties in a staggering show of consistency. More like it, right?

Sadly not. Rohit had a forgettable tour of South Africa in early 2018 and even though he made 37 and 63 not out in Adelaide and Melbourne, respectively, towards the end of the year, he was dropped from the Test XI for the next series in the Caribbean in August 2019. The two-Test series was India's first engagement in the newly constituted World Test Championship.

The Red-ball Opener Arrives

By this time, Mayank Agarwal had made the most of a mid-tour call-up to Australia by scoring 76, 42, 77 and 5 in his four knocks in Melbourne and Sydney, respectively, as India secured their maiden series victory Down Under. K.L. Rahul was given another opportunity to re-establish himself as a Test opener after having lost his place to his great friend Agarwal in Australia, but he didn't have a great time in the Caribbean, only making 44, 38, 13 and 6 in India's 2-0 series triumph.

It was during this series that Kohli and Shastri put into motion a plan that would alter the landscape of Indian cricket. Rohit was coming off a spectacular 50-over World Cup with five centuries and with India still to nail down an established opening pair, the idea of thrusting Rohit up the order in red-ball cricket too started to take shape. Rohit batted a lot in the nets against the new ball in preparation for India's next Test challenge, a three-match home showdown against South Africa, in October.

The challenge of undertaking a new role in Test cricket energized him and Rohit understood that the management group was going out on a limb to back him. In an interview with Jatin Sapru* on the latter's YouTube channel, Rohit was effusive in his thanksgiving to Shastri and Kohli for their faith in him and his abilities. 'I was very grateful to Ravi Shastri and Virat Kohli for giving me the opportunity to bat up the order. It wasn't an easy decision to promote me in Tests.

---

*Sapru, Jatin, 'Rohit Sharma's UNFILTERED Chat with Jatin Sapru', *YouTube*, 7 June 2024, https://tinyurl.com/3rjy8z36, Accessed on 20 February 2025.

They trusted me,' he said. 'They asked me to play one practice match, which I did. I got out on the very first ball, but I realized that I didn't have any other choice. It felt like a second birth in Test cricket. I knew I had to grab this opportunity, whether it meant opening, batting at number five or six, or even lower down the order.

'My response to them was clear—I'll play my natural game and won't take the pressure of trying to survive. I'm going to play freely. If the ball is there, whether it's the first ball of the Test or not, I'm going to hit it. They gave me the freedom to do what I wanted.'

So it was that some four years after Shastri first broached the subject of Rohit opening in Tests, the move actually fructified. At the time, in 2015, Shastri was the director of the team and Kohli had just taken over as full-time captain. 'Ravi *bhai* was very eager for me to open in Tests for a long time. He told me in 2015 that I should consider it as an option,' Rohit further revealed. 'He wanted me to open, but the decision wasn't in my hands.'

In many ways, the South Africa series was make-or-break for Rohit's future as a Test batter. It was during that home series that Vikram Rathour took over as India's batting coach. Sanjay Bangar had occupied that role for five years until the end of the World Cup when Rathour, himself a former Test opener, replaced him. 'When I joined the team (after the West Indies tour),' he says, 'the discussion (about Rohit opening in Tests) was already going on. The idea was Ravi's. Rohit was batting phenomenally well in white-ball cricket at the time. He was really, really good, looking in great touch. And I agreed with that (the move to promote him). A player like him should be played in whatever number. He was too good a player to be missing out on any cricket that India was playing.

'Ravi thought opening should be good for him and so we started with him. The rest is, as they say, history. Rohit is the kind of player who looks after himself. There were hardly any technical inputs that he was looking for; he mostly had his game sorted. At times, he'll want you to look out for something, if he's making a change, or he'll come and have a discussion, a kind of validation about whatever he's thinking. But for the South African series, we didn't work on any technical stuff. He just opened, batted really well, scored some big runs.'

Rohit's first Test as opener in Visakhapatnam, at the same ground where his Test charge had stymied three years ago, yielded scores of 176 and 127. Both were magnificent efforts, free-flowing and without self-doubt or inhibition. He was a natural fit at the top of the tree in Test matches too, a fact he would reinforce a fortnight later with 212 in the final Test in Ranchi.

Agarwal was Rohit's first opening partner in Tests and their maiden foray in the first innings in Visakhapatnam netted 317 runs. 'He was just so calm and collected,' says Agarwal—who himself slammed 215—of Rohit in the build-up to the Test. 'It looked like he had really thought about a game plan that he had in his mind with regard to how he wanted to go about playing that series, how he would approach it as an opening batsman. It felt like he had a lot of clarity.

'He was very sure; he was just the Rohit that we all know—jovial and doing his things, preparing in the way that

The Rise of the Hitman

he usually prepares. Even when we were batting in the middle, we were just talking about game plans and he stuck to the plan. Standing at the non-striker's end, I knew he was going about doing his thing—playing (Kagiso) Rabada, (Vernon) Philander in a particular manner, very close to his body, waiting for them to really come close to the stumps. He looked to play them with a little bit of caution. And then, once the spinners came on, he opened up. That actually tells me a lot about how he had prepared and what sort of plan he had for him being an opener in Test cricket.'

Agarwal is amazed by the entire Rohit persona. 'He is a leader. He is somebody who really thinks a lot about the game,' he pipes in. 'I know he is perceived very differently, but he is somebody who actually sits and thinks a lot about the game. And does a lot of planning—not just for himself and about his own game, but he looks at other people and other people's game as well and then tries to see what he can take out of it or how he can help them.

'He is a lot of fun to bat with. You can sort of see that ease, you can sort of see that calm in him. He goes about playing his game like nothing much is happening. We all know that Rohit has got that extra bit of time when he plays. And it didn't feel any different when he initially opened the batting. It also helps when he is set and the opposition knows he is looking to take them down. That works really well. Under pressure, the opposition's plans go haywire and that also makes batting a lot easier for the partner batting with him, whoever it may be. The pace of the game really goes up.'

Indian cricket history is replete with numerous happy

accidents—Shastri opening in the final Test of the India-Pakistan series in 1982–83, Tendulkar moving up the white-ball order in New Zealand in 1994, and of course, Rohit opening in limited-overs cricket in 2013. This wasn't an accident *per se*, but for someone who had averaged 39.62 across 27 Tests in the middle order, to be asked to open six years after his debut and to make a grand fist of it falls right at the top of the list of inspired decision-making.

'I will tell you what, it's so easy for an individual not seeing things coming out of himself. By that I mean Rohit Sharma might not have even given a thought to being an opener in Test cricket,' W.V. Raman observes. 'He would have been looking at how to make runs in Test cricket. "Hey, am I doing that right, am I not doing this right?" That's what would have been going through his head.

'But if you had a guy who has been the most versatile of persons, who has done it at the topmost level and who is also very sort of authoritative when he says something and also very motivational when he tells you, and he reinforces the fact that, trust me, trust my cricketing experience, you will succeed if you open, it changes the perspective of the individual,' Raman continues, speaking of the Shastri effect. 'That's exactly what was needed for Rohit at that time. Fortunately, he had somebody like Ravi and also a captain who bought that idea.

'That's something that we don't really highlight. I also think that him opening and succeeding would have also helped him realize that there are things that he needs to try in order to see how well he can succeed. Maybe that is one particular trigger that helped him become a better captain as well. He would have felt, "*Arre, abhi tak* I have not tried this. Now, how am I to know if it is a good move or not?" That perhaps encouraged him to try things out as captain and see if it worked or not.'

Raman has been a huge Rohit backer for a long time and feels that one of the things that held him back as a Test cricketer was the lack of sustained, consistent opportunities. 'From the outside, I always felt there was a little bit of that indecision going around in his case. With him too, maybe, but mainly from team managements not being certain about him. He also was not looking at other options than being a middle-order batter in Test cricket. But once Ravi felt that the top of the order is where he needs to try and be, that little push was something that he needed.

'Once he got that, he too perhaps knew that he had reached a point of no-return,' Raman goes on. 'Opening in Test cricket, he realized he had to make it work. And he said, "Yes, if I can be aggressive, get runs in One-Day cricket, why can't I do it in Test cricket?" It's a question of the mindset. One of the things that he has started doing differently since opening in Test cricket is going after the short delivery and that's something which has really worked well for him. That's also made him a bit of a serious threat for the fast bowlers who could otherwise scare batters with the short stuff. They've got to think twice now, thrice in fact, because he can power it into the stands without any problem.'

There were many who felt, from 2014 to the middle of 2019, that Rohit might be lost to Test cricket; that he wouldn't touch the dizzy heights his talent almost demanded. Ajit Agarkar doesn't fall entirely in that category, though he admits, 'You always worry. You hope not, because luckily, age was on his side at that point. And he had established himself as a really good white-ball player. But it's not like the game is going to stop for you just because you are talented. So, you worry about it. That's why I feel it would have been a disappointment if he had not achieved what he has today.

'That sort of talent is very rare. But with that talent, you need a lot of hard work. And whether you take Rahul Dravid or Sachin, I've known him closely, he is one of the most talented players to ever play the game. But Sachin worked as hard as he possibly could. If someone as talented as Sachin has to put in that work, then everyone else has to.

'And that's what Rohit did. I'm glad he did so, especially in Test cricket. I don't think in One-Day cricket or T20s there was ever going to be a real issue. But to make it in Test cricket, whether captaincy has helped him, he'll probably be the best person to answer. I'm glad whoever made that decision to get him to open, did it at that stage.'

Response to Critics

Rohit's elevation as Test opener wasn't quite welcomed with open arms by all the connoisseurs, who felt that he was too flashy and played too many strokes too early in his innings—recipes for disaster against the moving red ball. But he pleasantly surprised the doubters with his discipline and shot-selection, willing to grind it out if the situation demanded, as it most certainly did in England in 2021. Kumble, who had had a first-hand view of Rohit's resurrection until his untimely injury in Visakhapatnam, acknowledges that Rohit surpassed his expectations in his new avatar.

'I was surprised with his adaptability to opening the innings in Test matches,' Kumble says, clearly impressed by how well Rohit had taken to the demanding role. 'We all know him as a great player—but to adapt to the red ball in Test matches, I didn't expect him to slip into it as effortlessly as he did in his white-ball opening role. Suddenly, he became very destructive and everybody feared him when he walked in to bat (in limited-overs games). I didn't expect that to happen naturally in a red-ball contest. I thought he would find it difficult because of the moving ball, especially early on in his innings in conditions like England and maybe South Africa or New Zealand.

'But he seems to have really adapted to that role very well. He was around 32 when he made the move to open the batting in Tests. To be able to do that speaks, apart from ability, also of a lot of mental resilience. He is also the ultimate team player, right? At the end of it, you need to be a good team player to adapt to any situation. If you are so strung up about your position in the line-up, the messaging is that "Look, I want to look after myself." That's how I see it,' Kumble insists. 'When people are so strung up about certain positions in the batting order because that's where they have always played and they're not happy to be shunted up and down, then it's letting the team down. When someone is flexible and open to batting out of position, then you know that this guy has the mental capability to adapt. Of course, you turn to a player like that because you know that that particular player has the skill and the ability to adapt, but more importantly, the individual himself has to have that mindset of doing it for the team. That's what was very evident with Rohit and that's one of the reasons why I think he succeeded in all formats as a batter. I also feel that's one of the key reasons why players respect him immensely as a captain.'

Rohit ended up with 529 runs from three Tests against South Africa, marking his maiden series as opener as an unqualified success. Against Bangladesh, in the two subsequent Tests the following month, he only made 6 and 21, but that was almost incidental as India swept to a 2-0 victory.

India were done with their Test engagements for the calendar year. In 2020, they would embark on a full tour of New Zealand where the two Tests at the conclusion of the white-ball leg would be Rohit's first serious examination as opener against the seaming, swinging red ball. Rohit was itching to get going and test himself in demanding conditions. But even he didn't know at the conclusion of the November 2019 pink-ball Test against Bangladesh in Kolkata that his next Test appearance wouldn't be for another 13 and a half months.

9

Acing the English Test

Two days before 2019 dawned, Rohit welcomed his first child—daughter Samaira. He flew back home after the Melbourne Test victory in December 2018 and missed the final, New Year's Test in Sydney, which India drew to clinch their first series victory in Australia. Towards the middle of the year, he slammed an unmatched five centuries in a single 50-over World Cup and had secured the Test opening slot by the end of October. There was so much to look forward to in 2020.

At least that was the expectation.

India kicked off their tour of New Zealand in January 2020 with a comprehensive 5-0 sweep in the Twenty20 Internationals, two of those victories coming via the Super Over. After a tepid start, Rohit hit his straps with 65 in the third game in Hamilton and eased to 60, batting at number three, in the final outing in Mount Maunganui, when he was forced to retire hurt with a calf injury that ended his participation in the tour.

It was perhaps mere coincidence that once Rohit returned

Brothers-in-arms—two legends, one trophy, a billion dreams fulfilled

Years of sacrifice, countless battles, one ultimate embrace—mission accomplished

Smiles, silverware, and a story of sheer dominance. Leading from the front, bringing glory home…

The dream, the grind, the ultimate prize—Rohit gazing at the trophy that a country was awaiting with bated breath for 13 years

Where battles were fought and dreams realized—Rohit paying tribute to the pitch that helped rewrite history...

Hands on the craft, eyes on the ball—Rohit has always been the master of timing

Elegance, power and precision in one frame—Rohit sending it soaring with his signature pull shot

Grace meets might—Rohit with another effortless stroke

Pulling no punches—if there is one stroke that defines Rohit, it is this, it is this, it is this…

Poetry in motion—'Hitman' at work, an image for the ages

Cut out for greatness—in the mood, Rohit shines brighter than the floodlights

home, India failed to win a single match, surrendering the ODIs 0-3 and the Tests 0-2. Not long after that tour ended, the Covid-19 pandemic broke out and brought the world to a standstill. One of the minor fallouts of the pandemic was the postponement of IPL 2020 which would eventually be held in the United Arab Emirates between 19 September and 10 November.

Back in Action after the Pandemic: IPL, Brisbane Test and WTC Final

The prolonged lockdown in India between March and May prevented the players from adhering to their uncompromising fitness routines. Perhaps because of that, or perhaps not, Rohit sustained a hamstring strain in his left leg during an IPL game on 18 October, which ruled him out of play for four matches over the next two weeks. Consequently, he initially wasn't picked for any of India's squads for the long multi-format tour of Australia that would commence immediately after the IPL.

Rohit was back in action on 3 November and emphatically laid all doubts to rest with 68 in the final against Delhi Capitals which Mumbai Indians won by five wickets to retain their title. By now, he had earned a ticket to Australia, though he wouldn't be declared 'international cricket-ready' until 7 January 2021, for the third Test in Sydney, with the series locked at 1-1.

After the disastrous 36 all out in the first day-night Test in Adelaide, India regrouped magnificently under Ajinkya Rahane once Virat Kohli returned home on paternity leave. The stand-in captain inspired a stirring comeback in the second Test in

The Rise of the Hitman

Melbourne with a majestic century, rocking Australia, who believed that once India lost Kohli and Mohammed Shami (broken forearm) after their hammering in the first Test, the series was all but destined to end in their favour.

India lost Ravindra Jadeja during the Melbourne victory but welcomed Rohit back for Sydney and he didn't disappoint, grinding out 26 in the first innings and 52 in the second. Hanuma Vihari and R. Ashwin braved back and hamstring injuries, respectively, to earn a miraculous draw and leave the series squared at 1-1 going into the final match in Brisbane, where Australia hadn't lost for more than three decades.

By the Brisbane Test, which started on 15 January 2021, India had lost more than half the side that had started the series in Adelaide. Apart from Kohli and Shami, Vihari, Ashwin, all-rounder Jadeja (dislocated thumb) and pace-ace Jasprit Bumrah (abdominal injury) were also missing. It was time for the few remaining seniors to stand up. Rohit battled hard whilst making 44 in the first innings but was dismissed for just seven in the second when India were set a record 328 for an epochal victory. Rishabh Pant's heroic unbeaten 89 crowned an epic triumph, a memorable comeback that earned India inarguably their greatest series triumph overseas—perhaps of all time.

Within three weeks of their return home, India were locked in a titanic battle with England as they chased a berth in the final of the inaugural World Test Championship. They had to win at least three of the four games but got off to the worst start imaginable, losing at home for the first time since 2017 in the first of two Tests in Chennai. Rohit took it upon himself to set the tone in the second, smashing a jaw-dropping 161 in the first innings to set up a commanding victory, then bossing the dicey tracks in Ahmedabad, which hosted the last two games, with scores of 66, 25 not out, and 49. A second successive series victory, after going 0-1 down, was rewarded with a shot at New Zealand in the WTC final in Southampton, and even though Rohit got off to a good start in both innings—with 34 and 30—he couldn't kick on and India were well beaten by eight wickets.

The English Test

The WTC final ended on 23 June and the first of India's five Tests against England, in Nottingham, wasn't until 4 August. Given the strict quarantine rules in place, the team chose to not return home. Players were left to their own devices for three weeks, though they had to update the authorities of the results of their lateral flow tests every few days. England had partially opened up from 21 June, but it wasn't until 19 July that life returned to a semblance of the normalcy of the pre-Covid phase.

The members of the Indian squad reassembled in their London hotel on 13 July and left for Durham the following day for their final preparations ahead of the Test series. It was in Durham that the seeds for Rohit's remarkable run in the England Tests were sowed.

'Rohit was on a mission to realign his approach towards opening the batting in Tests,' R. Sridhar, who watched him from the closest quarters possible, says. 'There was a lot of self-introspection. He had got out to Kyle Jamieson in the

The Rise of the Hitman

WTC final, reaching out to a wide ball, which didn't amuse him. He therefore made a conscious and significant technical adjustment. Rohit changed the way he picked up the bat, he changed his backswing. He made sure he cocked his wrist, he ensured his bat was close to the body. The adjustment was so drastic that he hurt his left wrist, but because he was keeping the hands as they were in his stance, he came down softly on the ball. That allowed him to focus on timing, not hitting the ball. It also helped him leave the ball better.

'The very fact that deep down within him he wanted to make a name for himself in Test cricket and was willing to put in the hard yards required to do so was brilliant. The discipline he showed in making the change was exemplary. The most important thing was unlearning what he had learnt. Unlearning and relearning in that Durham camp within two weeks was a phenomenal effort from Rohit.'

In his capacity as batting coach, Vikram Rathour worked tirelessly with Rohit, ensuring that he gave the opener all the tools required to succeed in the series to follow. Rathour was immediately struck by Rohit's determination to establish himself as an opener in England—he was also yet to score a Test hundred outside India, batting at any position.

'He was really, really keen to do well there because...,' notes Rathour, 'he thought that that is the real test of him opening. Getting runs in India is okay—I think he felt at times it's easier to score runs when opening in India. But he was really keen to do well in England. That is when he started working on certain things. He wanted to play the ball closer to the body, he didn't want the hands to get away from the body, things like that.

'I was just looking out for him when he was batting in the nets. One of his other concerns at times was the timing of his initial movement. If he was moving too late or too early, the movement used to be too big, where he would go to the off-stump sometimes, sometimes even beyond off-stump, with his back-and-across shuffle. Those were the things we would work on to ensure that his back-and-across movement wasn't too pronounced and that he kept his hands closer to the body and played the ball late, under his head.'

While the technical changes helped, Rathour is also of the view that it was in making the mental adjustments that Rohit was in a class of his own. 'Technically, he was always a very sound player,' Rathour says. 'The biggest change he had to bring in was mental. To play with the kind of discipline he showed in England—when you play through a session, scoring 30 or 35 runs, that is not the way Rohit plays. That's not something that comes naturally to him. For me, I think that was his biggest achievement—that he could bring in that change and be as disciplined as he wanted to be.

'*That*, and the conviction that "I need to do this to score runs in England." Having that conviction and thinking along those lines is one thing, but to be able to do that is completely different. Of course, he showed that he could. He was also willing to do whatever the team required him to do. He's a huge team man; that is where all the success has come through.'

Armed with a refined technique and a grim determination that wasn't always associated with him even at this stage of his career, Rohit struck up an excellent opening tandem with K.L. Rahul, his partner for most of the 2019 World Cup in the same country. The tone was set in Nottingham, during the drawn first Test, when the two added 97 and 34 in the two innings. In the second Test at Lord's, they ramped it up a notch by putting on 126 in the first innings, with Rahul's 129 and the pacers' brilliance in the second innings setting up a magnificent victory to put India 1-0 up.

Rohit made 36, 12 not out, 83 and 21 in the first four innings of the series, missing out on a maiden overseas ton in the Lord's first innings, when he was bowled by a beauty from James Anderson that nipped back sharply on pitching and burst through the gate. He then produced a second-innings half-century in a losing cause in Leeds. So, when the teams went to The Oval for the fourth Test, his quest for a first ton away from home was still to be fulfilled.

The Oval is renowned to be a batting paradise but things were different this time around. Chris Woakes and Ollie Robinson made the most of the conditions to skittle India for 191 after Joe Root won the toss. England escaped from 62 for five to open up a 99-run lead, leaving India to do all the heavy lifting if they weren't to fall behind going into the decider in Manchester.

India needed Rohit and Rahul to rediscover their mojo after the disappointing starts of 1, 34 and 28 in their previous three outings. The two classy right-handers had set the tone in the first two Tests and their inability to see off the new ball had been one of the reasons for team totals of 78 and 278 all out in Leeds, and 191 in the first dig at The Oval. Now trailing by 99, the openers had to pitch in for India to stay in touch.

Rohit and Rahul responded admirably by stitching

together 83. Watchful and risk-free, they took 34 overs in doing so. But no one was complaining. Time wasn't a factor; it was all about runs on the board. Having bedded down, Rohit wasn't going to throw it away this time. In Cheteshwar Pujara, he found another willing ally as India eased past the deficit and built a handy lead.

Rohit worked his way into the 80s, but once there, he was not going to linger any longer. Two sweeps off Moeen Ali's off-spin, followed by a crunching pull off Anderson, took him to within a stroke of his century and he got there in style, imperiously depositing Moeen over long-on for his first six. It was an emphatic way to get to three-figures off 204 deliveries; his second half-century had taken just 60 balls as he worked through the gears. Rohit finally had a Test hundred on foreign soil after having scored seven of them at home. Only Mominul Haque (ten), Allan Lamb (nine) and Mahela Jayawardene (eight) had more tons at home before scoring one overseas.

There was equal parts relief and delight, but Rohit wasn't caught up in the moment. He batted on to make 126, spanning nearly six hours, when he perished to the first delivery with the second new cherry, top-edging a pull to the only man behind square on the on-side. It was a disappointing end to a spectacular display—the timing of the dismissal equally galling—but his 153-run stand with Pujara had put India on the ascendancy. Further half-centuries from Rishabh Pant and Shardul Thakur pushed India to 466 and set England a target of 368, well beyond them against India's quality bowling attack. Bowled out for 210, England went down by 157 runs to help India surge to a 2-1 advantage.

The Rise of the Hitman

The teams travelled to Manchester for what ought to have been the fifth and final Test, but with a Covid outbreak in the Indian ranks and the fear of what might be, that game was postponed. It wouldn't be another ten months before that Test was played in Birmingham in July 2022. Rohit (by now the all-format captain) missed the game due to Covid and India lost by seven wickets—the series ending 2-2—leaving everyone to wonder what might have been had the final game been played as scheduled in Manchester, with India carrying both momentum and form.

Rohit finished those four Tests in 2021 with 368 runs—India's highest scorer. He averaged 52.57, but more importantly, his strike-rate was 42.49, which testified to the price he put on his wicket, the methods he adopted to give himself the best chance of success in difficult conditions and the efficacy of those methods in a stunning presentation of mind over matter. Rohit Sharma was no longer an accidental Test opener; indeed, by September 2021, within 22 months of his first shot at opening the batting, he was among the best Test opening batters of the time.

'To go up against a really good attack in Anderson and (Stuart) Broad, among others, in testing conditions and to do well, I'm sure that would have changed the course of his mindset more than his career,' Ajit Agarkar affirms. 'He was still a terrific white-ball player at that point. But I'm glad he is where he is in Test cricket today. The mental resolve… If you talk to him today or to the other guys who have worked with him or played with him, they will tell you how driven he is.

'He might sometimes come across as lazy in his approach.

But the heart and the mind are in the right place to do well for India and to take the Indian team to different heights. That is the evolution you want to see. Maybe it's happened a little bit late in Test cricket, when he found his spot at the top. But that England series, just the way that he batted... The mental resolve he showed for someone who's such a natural shot-maker, that was nice to see. It would have been a shame for someone with that kind of talent not to have a great Test career. Hopefully, he's still got a long way to go.

'But at least over the last three or four years in Test cricket, he's made a name for himself. If that had not happened, it would have been a little bit of a disappointment for me, having seen him as a player very closely,' Agarkar adds.

V.V.S. Laxman knows a thing or two about batting out of position in Test cricket. The Hyderabadi made his debut in 1996 against South Africa in Ahmedabad at number six, and made a crucial 51 in the second innings in India's 64-run win. But four months later, he was forced to open the batting, for the first time in his life, against West Indies in Kingston. Even though he made 64 in his first act as opener, it wasn't a position he was comfortable with. After grappling with that slot for three years and 14 Tests, with mixed results, he informed the selectors that he was through with opening, even if it meant he would have to miss Test cricket.

'I know by experience that it's tough (for a middle-order batter to open in Tests),' Laxman points out. 'But even then, it didn't look like Rohit was playing for his place. In conditions where you almost expect him not to do well, whether it's in England or even Australia—tough conditions, good bowling

The Rise of the Hitman

attacks—you don't expect a number six batter like Rohit to do well as an opener. But he looked in control because of the work he put in. For example, he understood that a good start is essential for the team to do well in England. You know that the opening stand is very important. One of the keys to succeeding there is leaving the ball. Rohit worked out that leaving balls outside off was something he had to do for the sake of the team, and I feel that he went out of his way to change his natural game.

'It is very difficult for a player of the calibre of Rohit to do that. It is very, very tough for a natural stroke-player, who has so many double-hundreds in ODIs, to control his bat and his hands. But he did that for the team and that is something he is continuing to do even as a captain. In the last two years, since he has become the captain, you see the example he is setting. He is walking the talk, as they say—"This is what I want from the batters and I am showing you how to do it." But that has always been there with him. It is not something he has acquired just because he has become the captain.'

Laxman attributes Rohit's growth as a fabulous leader to his innate desire to do what's always best for the team. 'When you are a captain, when you are the leader, what do your players see? Is he playing for himself? Or is he trying to set an example as to how one should play for a team?' Laxman asks rhetorically. 'And when they can see that whatever you are doing is for the team, you don't have to tell them anything after that.'

Deconstructing the Rohit technique that has allowed him to flourish as a Test opener, Laxman notes, 'He has really, really impressed me. At the beginning of his career, and even in the middle stages before he started to open, the area where he was susceptible against the right-arm fast bowler was outside the off-stump, because he would seldom move his foot to the pitch of the ball. He would plant his left foot—you know, just a small, short step—and it was more about using his hands. Because of that, with that movement, he used to offer a lot of catches to the slip cordon area, or he would get caught in the backward point region by playing a little early. But that has changed. That series in England is where that change happened, where he knew precisely where his off-stump was.

'Suddenly, Rohit, the aggressive opener, started to be a little more circumspect. He was very clear where his off-stump was and he was willing to leave the ball. But that doesn't mean that he was not playing his shots. His game plan was very clear and he worked out what his scoring areas against the new ball were. Once the ball got old, he started to play his normal game.

'But against the new ball, as an opener, especially in overseas conditions, he was quick to understand what his scoring areas were and which were the areas he required to be careful about. Anything which was in the channel (outside off), he was ready to leave on the front foot. But anything which he could play off the back foot, he still went back and played the punch beautifully.'

Laxman is of the view that, because of his strong grounding in backfoot play, Rohit was able to access various parts of the ground. 'He is someone who can play the cut shot really well—he is a very good puller. The moment the ball was aimed at his body, he'd use his wrists and pull or also play the on-drive and the flick. His game plan became very clear to him, he had the conviction to follow that.

'When he opened and got off to that kind of start, with two centuries and a double in his first three Tests in that role, it was no longer about establishing himself but about how he could contribute and play "impact knocks", not worry about milestones and individual accomplishments. It was all about "How can I destroy the bowling attack?" Destroy not just by playing his shots, but also by driving them to distraction with his "leaves", like in England. That was his mindset, even if many felt being asked to open the Test batting was almost a last throw of the dice so far as Rohit was concerned.'

That England series became Rohit's defining moment as a Test opener. The discipline he portrayed while leaving balls, the responsibility he embraced in providing the starts that his confidence demanded, and the willingness to go against his natural grain, endeared him all over again to even diehard backers of the past, of whom W.V. Raman was one.

'It's been terrific, the way he has done things in the last five years at the top of the order, both in white-ball and red-ball cricket. That's something people expected that Sourav (Ganguly, the former India captain) would do,' Raman says. 'Because he was so fluent in the limited-overs format at the top of the order, they felt he might fill in when they were looking for Test openers. Sourav refused, but that's something Rohit has done, and done really well.

'Opening in white-ball cricket is completely different from opening in red-ball cricket. But Rohit has erased that difference out of batting. How has he done that? By being fluent, by being the same stroke-maker that he was at number five or number six. Normally, you tend to see batters play a lot of shots in white-ball cricket as an opener because the fielders are inside the circle, the Powerplay restrictions are in place and the mandate is to go and get runs. But what Rohit has done is that he has also realized that there are a lot of gaps to be exploited even in red-ball cricket, so why not just pounce on any opportunity that comes his way. That's why you don't see him just hanging in there. And that's why I said that he doesn't make batting a laborious exercise.'

Like Laxman, Raman is also very impressed with how Rohit approached the 2021 England tour. 'For somebody who is a natural stroke-maker to give that first hour to the bowler, that was excellent,' Raman crows. 'Where he did things differently in that respect was not to reach out early on in his innings. He was waiting for the bowlers to bowl at him, I think this is something Ravi (Shastri) might have spoken to him about.

'That's something that he did well as an opener in red-ball cricket, making the bowlers bowl to him. Without your realizing, reaching out for balls becomes a habit when you are an opener in white-ball cricket. There is not much swing, not much seam and there is no dampness in the surface because you play day-night games. Generally, the ball skids on nicely. But in red-ball cricket, it is different.

'And that is the huge progression I have seen in Rohit in red-ball cricket, from his early, younger, inexperienced days to the current experienced version. The difference in England was that he was not going towards the ball, which obviously made

The Rise of the Hitman

the bowlers bowl short and try and see if he would get out to the hook shot. The hook shot is a 50-50 shot for most, it's not a stroke that always gives the odds to the batter. But Rohit is a master of the hook and the pull and when he made the bowlers bowl at him and bowl short, he took full toll. That was a great lesson in the art of manipulating the bowlers.'

There has been no looking back since that path-breaking England tour of 2021, though in his last two series, at home against New Zealand and away in Australia, he courted a terrible slump. Rohit has made another away Test hundred in Roseau against West Indies, in a 2023 series that fetched him 240 runs in just three innings. By adding this dimension to his batting, his is now one of the most coveted scalps in Test cricket too, a commendable feather in the cap of a supremely gifted batter whose long-format career appeared to have hit a crossroads not too long back.

10

The Leadership Masterstroke

Even though he retired abruptly from Test cricket towards the end of 2014—after a stonewalling rearguard display that helped India secure a draw in the Boxing Day Test against Australia—Mahendra Singh Dhoni wasn't entirely done with the international game. He played on till the 2019 World Cup in England and remained the white-ball captain until the start of the 2017 calendar year. By then, Virat Kohli had been the Test captain for two years and it was no surprise that he assumed the leadership role in the limited-overs formats as well.

Rohit's Test career was yet to take off at that stage, but in the two white-ball versions, he was in a league of his own and was a natural deputy to Kohli in the One-Day International and Twenty20 International squads. When Kohli was named the white-ball captain too, Rohit had already led Mumbai Indians to two IPL titles, in 2013 and 2015; within months of India welcoming their limited-overs skipper, Rohit had another IPL triumph in the summer of 2017.

Nonetheless, national captaincy wasn't immediately forthcoming.

First International Captaincy Stint

The first time Rohit led India was during Sri Lanka's tour of India in December 2017. As Kohli sat out the white-ball legs, Rohit captained the team in both the ODI and the T20I series. His international captaincy career got off to a disastrous start as he oversaw a seven-wicket loss to a Suranga Lakmal-inspired Sri Lanka in Dharamsala on 10 December. But retribution was swift and immediate. Rohit smashed an unbeaten 208, his third ODI double-ton, in the next outing in Mohali which India won comfortably. A commanding seven-wicket victory in Visakhapatnam, in the decider, gave India a 2-1 series score line, which they improved upon by sweeping the T20I series 3-0. Like in the preceding series, Rohit touched three-figures again in his second T20I as captain, smashing 118 in a mere 43 balls. He took just 35 deliveries to reach his hundred, which remains the fastest T20I ton by an Indian to date.

Rohit's reputation as a captain had already been well established by the time he took charge, if only on a temporary basis, of the white-ball sides in Kohli's absence. One of his earliest captaincy coups came in the three-nation Nidahas Trophy T20 tournament in Colombo in March 2018, where Bangladesh were the third team. After a tepid start, Rohit came into his own in the final league match against Bangladesh where his 61-ball 89 secured India's passage to the final against the same opponents four days later. In a tense title clash, where Rohit's 56 kept India in the race to hunt down Bangladesh's 166 for eight, the latter got their noses in front with the match going deep.

The Leadership Masterstroke

As India's required rate mounted, Rohit kept holding Dinesh Karthik back. By then, the wicketkeeper-batter had made a name for himself as a finisher, but Rohit seemed not to go by reputation, first sending Manish Pandey and then Vijay Shankar ahead of Karthik. By the time the irate Karthik, steam pouring out of his ears, was finally unleashed, the task looked beyond his and India's reach—34 needed in two overs.

Karthik felt he had a point to prove, smashing 16 off his first three deliveries and 22 in all from the penultimate over from Rubel Hossain. With 12 required off the last over, Shakib Al Hasan took a punt and summoned Soumya Sarkar's medium pace to the bowling crease. With his first five legal deliveries, Sarkar conceded only seven runs and took Shankar's wicket off the penultimate delivery, having him caught in the deep. In today's scenario, new batter Washington Sundar would have been on strike. But as the rules existed then, because the batters had crossed, Karthik would face the last ball of the final. Four would push the contest into a Super Over, six would mean an Indian victory against all odds.

Sarkar bowled full and outside off. Karthik held his shape and smashed him, flat and hard over the cover fence, for a six. It was an incredible stroke in any situation, but with so much hinging on that one ball, it was almost beyond belief. Still smouldering, Karthik was mobbed by his colleagues, Sarkar and Bangladesh slumped to the ground in agony, and the stands erupted, not because the Sri Lankans loved India more but because they had no fondness for the Bangladeshis.

'It was a very important tournament for Rohit,' Karthik remembers. 'It was in his nascent stages as a captain. Here was his opportunity, without the senior players, but against two good teams—Sri Lanka in Sri Lanka is always a good team, Bangladesh enjoys playing in Sri Lanka. In fact, they comfortably beat Sri Lanka to make the final. From India's point of view, none of the big names were there—no Dhoni, no (Jasprit) Bumrah, obviously no Virat Kohli. So it was a young team, a lot of young guys. That gave Rohit the chance to showcase his skills as a captain at the international level.

'How he backed them and how he got the best out of them, how tactical he was as a skipper—all of that came through very strongly in that tournament.'

Karthik wears an impish smile as he reflects on his ire at being held back by his good friend. 'The final was a place where I wanted to bat at a certain position, where I was batting throughout the tournament,' he says, with refreshing honesty. 'But he delayed my entry point. And when he did send me, I was upset, saying, why am I going so late? But when I got the job done, he explained the thought process behind it, as to why he held me back.'

Mustafizur Rahman, the left-arm pacer with a variety of slower deliveries, was to bowl the eighteenth over with India needing 35 for victory. India couldn't have won the game in that over but could so easily have lost it, which influenced Rohit's call to delay Karthik's entry to the middle. As it turned out, 'The Fizz' sent down a maiden—the only run that came off the over was a leg bye, and Pandey was caught at long-on off the last ball.

'Rohit told me that he felt that over of Mustafizur would be an important over where I could have tried to do a little extra and gotten out and the chances of winning the match would have reduced tremendously. As luck would have it, I was in the middle for the first ball of the nineteenth over and in hindsight, it was a great move.'

Karthik agrees that the trait of a good leader is knowing more about his players than the players themselves. 'I am 100 per cent convinced that good leaders know what to do, and at what time, to get the best out of their soldiers.'

Full-Time Captain

One wasn't sure when, or whether, the captaincy of at least the white-ball national sides would come to Rohit on a full-time basis. Kohli was going strong and showing no signs of slowing down and even though Rohit would have loved to lead on his own steam, he didn't lose any sleep over it. In any case, he had a Test career to resurrect, which he did with aplomb once he clambered to the top of the batting order. He decided that it was best for things to happen at their own pace because he had no control over any of it.

Kohli hit a prolonged lean patch with the bat across formats from the beginning of 2020. The run-machine of the previous five years went AWOL. The Covid-19 pandemic and fatherhood might or might not have had anything to do with it, but ahead of the delayed T20 World Cup in the UAE in October–November 2021, Kohli announced that he would step down from the 20-over captaincy at the end of India's World Cup campaign. The team had a run to forget, playing itself out of contention after the first two matches following losses to Pakistan (by ten wickets—the first time they had been beaten by Pakistan in *any* World Cup) and New Zealand. The decision-makers in the BCCI didn't see merit in having two separate leaders in the two different limited-overs formats, so they relieved Kohli of the ODI captaincy and handed over the reins of the white-ball sides to Rohit.

Within a couple of months, on the three-Test tour of South Africa in December 2021–January 2022, Kohli abdicated the Test captaincy throne as well, without warning. He had been in the hot seat for seven years and perhaps decided that it was time to move on. By then, Ravi Shastri, his mentor and influencer, had moved on from being the head coach and was replaced by Rahul Dravid. Rohit was now among the top openers in Test cricket too, while Ajinkya Rahane had gone on a downward spiral and was fighting to keep himself relevant. So, Rohit succeeding Kohli as the all-format captain was almost inevitable.

'Rohit Sharma is an Indian legend. We all know that. He is one of India's great captains, in the same league as Kapil Dev, Sourav Ganguly and Mahendra Singh Dhoni,' Yuvraj Singh proclaims. 'He is a very good thinker of the game. You saw how he won us that T20 final when everything seemed lost. He had kept two overs of Jasprit; he used those two overs brilliantly. Tactically, he is excellent—he's very calm under pressure. And after he became the captain, everybody has gotten a consistent run. That's because when he was in the team in his early days, he didn't get a consistent chance in one spot.

'He's a captain who's made Indian cricket secure. I feel, before that, guys were not secure in the team. He's made sure everybody is getting equal opportunities; that's the great thing about him as captain.'

Ajit Agarkar is convinced that Rohit's journey and the late blossoming, in a manner of speaking, have influenced his thinking as a captain and leader. 'I'm sure it has, especially because it's (the captaincy) come so late to him,' he points out. 'The one thing is that till you don't do it, you don't know whether you're good at it or not. But he was already leading Mumbai Indians at that point and had had a lot of success. The IPL is a high-pressure tournament; with a team as terrific as MI, you're expected to win every time you play.

'To have that kind of pressure, having a lot of different teams coming through, that's the one thing that probably doesn't happen with a lot of the young captains that come through now, because there's no time to play domestic cricket as such,' he goes on. 'Either they're leading their teams in the IPL or they're then becoming (India) captains. Rohit came with a little bit more experience. But yes, it was accidental. In white-ball cricket, he had already led a few times when Virat was not available, so maybe he tuned his mind to be ready to lead in white-ball cricket. And this came along and I think it was only a good thing because, by then, he had established himself as a batter in the team at the top of the order.'

Agarkar believes the captaincy has rejuvenated Rohit. 'This extra responsibility, some people thrive in it. Unfortunately, Rohit's one of those guys who's been labelled as having a laidback attitude to life, in a sense. But he's still driven, make no mistake. Maybe he can absorb that pressure a bit better. You've seen with Indian captains how much pressure there is, especially if you're one of the top players in the team. There's always pressure—not just with your own performance but with the team's too. There's no doubt that even though it came late, I'm glad the captaincy came to him because it's probably given him that extra little bit of lift and drive.

'He could have got to a stage of his career where then you just... Maybe—who knows?—you just start looking after your own batting at times. But now, he's looking after 14 other people or 15 other people. And I've not seen him not give every bit of what he has over the last year; you get to see that more closely when you're working together as captain and selector. We're glad that he's around and he's trying to guide some of the younger guys coming through. That can only be helpful to Indian cricket. Having interacted with him over the last year even more closely, you know how keen he is that India keep their pre-eminent place in Test cricket.'

Rohit has always been a people person. But, especially in Indian cricket, it is very rare for the overwhelming majority to not just respect the captain but positively like him—Tiger Pataudi was one such individual and Rohit falls in that same category—because it is said that, as a captain, if you manage to keep all your players happy, then at some level you are not doing your job.

'It's a very tough trait to have,' agrees Karthik. 'I don't think it's right for me to say he would have connected with everybody that he's captained. But I have to say, a majority of the people that he has played with, he has made an impact on, and they've all played for him at some point. That's the sign of a very good captain.'

W.V. Raman is recognized as one of the best thinkers of the game. He led Tamil Nadu and South Zone with distinction, played for India under Mohammad Azharuddin and Sachin Tendulkar, and has interacted with numerous other leaders from across disciplines all over the world. So he is perfectly positioned to analyze Rohit the captain. 'He is terrific,' Raman gushes. 'What has really helped him become the captain and the leader that he *is* is that he has gone through all the stages that a cricketer goes through. From being rated as one extremely talented who got off to a good start in white-ball cricket and then rated as somebody who would be the next big thing, suddenly things didn't happen. He had a delayed debut in Test cricket and then a lot of doubts came into people's mind—"is this boy just somebody who looks good on particular days? Can he deliver on a sustained basis?" Those kinds of doubts crept in. I think that's what has made Rohit Sharma the leader that he is, the captain that he is, because he knows everything that goes on in a player's mind.

'That is a quality a captain needs to have—empathy and the fact that he has gone through that himself. For example, Sachin knows just about everything about cricket that there is to know. But if you were to ask him to say what it is like to lose your place and make a comeback after two–three years, he won't obviously be aware of what it is a player goes through. He might have seen players go through it, but he hasn't actually experienced it himself. Whereas Rohit Sharma has done that. I have always felt that you need to have such kind of guys as captains, because they can understand the mindsets and also the insecurities and thought processes that go through cricketers' minds. That's how you get captains making great moves.'

Drawing a parallel with Mahendra Singh Dhoni, Raman continues, 'I read recently Shikhar Dhawan saying that M.S. backed him before an ICC tournament when he was not in the best of form. That's because M.S. has also gone through phases where things have not gone well. He knows what is required to address that. That is exactly what has made Rohit what he is today as a captain and as a leader.'

Raman rates Rohit as a wonderful tactician because he has delved into the past and learnt his lessons. 'He knows how he perhaps lost out on a few days because of not being in the right mindset, because of him not being aware of the tactical argument. That awareness was not there in his cricket on certain days. In the first half of his career, he was not as studious as he became later on. All these things make a player learn and that's what has happened to him as well,' Raman argues. 'It's not that you pick up everything instantly or that you are born with everything. You learn a lot as you go along. That's something that has happened in his case as well. Captains are not born, they can be made; they can become one. Even if you are a born leader, as some people like to think, if you are not prone to learning, you are going to slide. It's a case of stretch and grow. Otherwise, you will shrink.'

Rohit has espoused and portrayed a brand of cricket that has found resonance with the fans. Under Kohli, India were feisty and fiery; under Rohit, they are fearless and entertaining. It's no longer about not taking a backward step or giving it back to the opposition. India are determined to carve their own path, no matter how daunting the situation might appear. They are not willing to compromise on the positive style they have embraced, because they are secure in the knowledge that if they execute their plans to the best of their ability, there is no team in the world that can stop them. That security should not be mistaken for arrogance or cockiness; the very fact that Rohit has managed to convince his colleagues to look beyond individual achievements and focus wholeheartedly on the collective is a tribute to his man-management and persuasive skills.

Captaincy, the Rohit Sharma Way

One of the key factors that ruled Indian cricket, until maybe even a decade back, was the fear of losing. Especially going into away Tests, the first objective was to not lose the game; victory was almost an afterthought. That started to change under Kohli's captaincy as India strung together a pace attack which could give back as good as India got. Under Rohit, India haven't played a lot of overseas Tests—just eight at the end of the Australian tour of 2024–25—but there have been plenty of white-ball games away from home, including the last two T20 World Cups in Australia and the Americas, respectively.

Rohit is a hands-on captain who loves being part of all meetings—batters' meetings, bowlers' meetings, you name it. He isn't just an attendee but an active participant on all such occasions and is a huge believer in data and technology. It's not that he doesn't go with his gut feeling, instinct and intuition, but he likes to be armed with details on match-ups and micro-analytical aids that might give him even the slightest edge in this technology-driven era.

The Rise of the Hitman

The amount of time Rohit devotes to his teammates is something that awes V.V.S. Laxman. Ahead of the 2022 T20 Asia Cup in the UAE, a dress rehearsal for the World Cup in Australia a month later, Dravid contracted Covid and joined the team late; Laxman doubled up as the coach for the first few days. 'In those four days, he impressed me so much,' Laxman recalls. 'The time he invested, the effort he made to spend time with every player, with every bowler… You know, one of the best meetings I have been a part of is when all the batters got together. It was a great discussion, Rohit leading the way and everyone chipping in—be it Virat, Hardik, D.K., everyone contributed there. But Rohit was clearly the leader. It was almost like he was, as a coach, talking to them.

'I remember when I took over at the NCA (December 2021), Kuldeep Yadav was there, rehabilitating. Rohit took Kuldeep into the conference room and sat down with him for nearly an hour. After that interaction, Kuldeep told me, "Sir, this is exactly what I needed." And you know how Kuldeep's graph has soared after that.'

One of the other things that struck Laxman in Dubai was Rohit's clarity of thought. 'We were discussing the playing XI and he was very clear about what he wanted, who he wanted and why he wanted specific personnel. He was very clear about that, keeping in mind the T20 World Cup in Australia. During practice sessions, he would finish all his stuff—do his catching, do his batting—and then talk to the other players. It was great to see his involvement and the effort he was making to ensure that he is connecting with everyone. To me, that was fabulous.'

Agarkar is as amazed by Rohit's man-management skills

as his tactical acumen and astute strategizing. 'He's a friend to everyone in the team,' he says of the captain. 'In today's day and age, there's a lot more on everyone's plate where players are concerned, and particularly so if you are the captain. It's a different world with three formats now. Everyone's trying to juggle that, where you're good at. To then have a captain who actually is friends with everyone—I don't think there's anyone in the team who Rohit wouldn't go and have a meal with, which is very rare today.

'I've been involved with IPL teams, I have done a little bit of commentary; I can see people generally by themselves a lot more than perhaps in our time,' Agarkar observes. 'It's not a criticism; it's just the way it has evolved now. But he's still that guy; he's actually seen the other side of it. His head and heart are still very old school, which is a real benefit for him. He knows that you're judged on the success that you get playing for the country. I mean, IPL is just as important, or T20 cricket, franchise cricket, is just as important. And you still want to do well wherever you play.

'But at the end of the day, you're judged as a player in international cricket. And if you have a leader who understands that, and then pushes people to do that, then you know that the guys will naturally follow it. That's his biggest strength. He's the terrific guy that he's always been. From the time I started to get to know him in Ranji Trophy till today, he's not changed at all as a person, which is rare. We played together in the 2007 T20 World Cup. It's 17 years later now and to still not change your values or how you look at things… There have been many really good players who've been leaders. To still have one of those around, it helps, especially with the changing times. That's what he's trying to do—to try and pass on those same values to some of the younger guys who are probably exposed to a different culture. That makes our job (as selectors) a lot easier.'

To Anil Kumble, the standout feature of Rohit as captain is his honesty. 'He's extremely honest,' the former captain emphasizes. 'You can see that on the field itself—he'll just straightaway tell a player what he thinks. That's a great attribute to have. That, and the fact that he's a great team player. You can make that out from the way he goes about things. He leads from the front; he certainly walks the talk in terms of how he wants the team to play. He made that shift himself; it was very clear after the T20 World Cup (semifinal) loss in Australia in 2022 that the shift had to be made, and he did that as the captain by not just asking his players to make it but by himself leading from the front.

'That attribute of managing a set of players who are extremely competitive and extremely skilful—managing them with a very jovial, relaxed approach—says a lot about him. The one thing that is very evident is his honesty and you can make out on the field that his emotions are all very, very genuine. He says it like it has to be said, he doesn't hold back but he says it without malice or ill-will and that's what has endeared him to everyone.'

Each skipper has their own methodology and there is no set template that everyone can follow. Rohit's unique combination of empathy and tough love has worked wonders; he has made the senior members of the team feel secure because he himself is far from insecure, and he has allowed the younger players

The Leadership Masterstroke

under him to blossom and take wings because he has given them the licence to go and express themselves without being shackled by the fear of failure.

'See, captaining is one thing, leading is another thing altogether,' Laxman explains patiently. 'For me, it is very important for a captain to have that connect with every player. That's why I am not surprised that they play for him. Everyone knows that he is the one that keeps the dressing room light, keeps the dressing room relaxed. At the same time, he will not tolerate nonsense. Even in team meetings, he can be decisive in shooting suggestions down if he feels they are not aligned with the team's philosophy. For him, it has ultimately been about the team, always.'

It's hard to believe sometimes that Rohit has only been India's all-format captain since early 2022. He has already led India to the finals of showpiece events in all three formats—the World Test Championship, the 50-over World Cup and the T20 World Cup, capping it off with another title tilt at the Champions Trophy. The first two ended in great disappointment—the second one particularly so after India mounted an extraordinary campaign right up until the final—but the third time was the charm for Rohit and India, and the fourth mirrored the triumph of the third. That alone will cement his legacy as one of India's great leaders, though it is evident that Rohit has more going for him than just the World Cup crown, no matter how desperately it was sought after in June 2024, and the Champions Trophy, where India rewrote history by becoming the first three-time winners.

11

Untold Agony, Unmatched Ecstasy

India had co-hosted the 50-over World Cup thrice before—in 1987, 1996 and 2011—but 2023 was the first time the tournament would be played entirely in India. The opening match, between defending champion England and New Zealand on 5 October, as well as the grand final on 19 November were to be held at the gargantuan Narendra Modi Stadium in Ahmedabad, also the venue for the event's marquee clash between India and Pakistan.

Race against Time: Injuries and Expectations

Rohit's team was in a desperate race against time, awaiting the return from injuries of wicketkeeper-batter K.L. Rahul (thigh) and middle-order kingpin Shreyas Iyer (back). Both had undergone surgeries in the summer and their progress was encouraging enough for the selectors to name them in a provisional 15-man World Cup squad in September, even as the team was engaged in a fierce battle with their continental rivals for the Asia Cup in Sri Lanka.

Rahul joined the team in Colombo a week into the tournament—having also overcome a groin strain—and made an immediate impact with a century against Pakistan in the second stage, but Iyer's comeback was stymied after just two preliminary outings in Pallekele. India were determined to give the Mumbaikar as much time as required to regain full fitness and Iyer responded with a century in India's penultimate ODI before the World Cup, against Australia in Indore, a foretaste of what was to come in the showpiece extravaganza.

The team was aware of the weight of expectations it carried but Rohit was determined to ensure that it was used as a spur and not regarded as a millstone. When the squad reached Thiruvananthapuram for their scheduled second and final official warm-up tie against Netherlands—abandoned without a ball bowled—Rohit assembled the support group for a meeting that was to play a stellar role in the events that unfolded.

The group included not just the cricket coaching staff but also everyone who was a non-playing part of the squad. Rohit's message was simple but significant—they had to function as a team, but with full freedom. 'This isn't about the players alone,' he told them. 'I want my support engine to be on point. I will be accessible to everyone at all times. If there is an issue, let me know and I will help resolve it. We will be travelling the length and breadth of the country. The expectations will be immense. Let's enjoy that. Let's soak all that in because this opportunity doesn't come often. But once we hit the ground, whether it is for a training session or a match, it must be only about the cricket and the responsibilities surrounding it that we need to fulfil.'

His words hit home because this was a new experience for the non-coaching staff. Then and there, seated in a circle, they felt that they had gone from being a cricket team to an extended family.

The 2023 Campaign Begins

Clearly, Rohit had drilled the same message into his 14 teammates, because the camaraderie on and off the field was obvious. India survived a mini-hiccup in the opener against Australia in Chennai—Virat Kohli and Rahul coming to the rescue after a horror start to a modest chase—and grew in stature as they played exhilarating, entertaining cricket with their captain in the forefront.

This was a team effort in every sense of the term. Contributions came from all quarters. When Shubman Gill was forced to miss the first two outings due to dengue, reserve wicketkeeper Ishan Kishan stepped in to fill the breach. He was out without scoring against the Aussies but played his part in a 156-run opening stand with Rohit in the next match against Afghanistan in Delhi. The first indication of the mayhem Rohit would inflict for the rest of the tournament came in this game as the captain blasted 16 fours and five sixes and raced to 131 off 84 deliveries. Rohit had laid down the marker. As subsequent events would prove, this wasn't a false dawn.

India worked through the draw with tremendous elan. There were handsome runs through the order and the bowling ticked over nicely with Jasprit Bumrah doing the damage up front and spinners Kuldeep Yadav and Ravindra Jadeja holding their own in the middle stages. Perennial bunnies Pakistan were swatted aside in Ahmedabad and India moved to Pune for their fourth outing against pesky neighbours Bangladesh, comfortably perched on top of the round-robin table.

Some 40 minutes into the game, Rohit brought his deputy Hardik Pandya on to bowl the ninth over with the Bangladeshis on 37 without loss. Liton Das drove the all-rounder's third ball back past the bowler and Pandya instinctively struck his left foot out on his follow-through. He immediately went down with a twisted ankle. After lengthy treatment, he attempted to bowl again but just could not put any weight on his left leg and hobbled off the ground. He would not play in the tournament again.

Pandya was supposed to be the fulcrum of the team, lending balance with his blistering ball-striking and more-than-brisk fast-medium. He was two cricketers rolled in one and when he was ruled out for the rest of the competition, India had to act decisively. That they did by placing their eggs in the specialists' basket. Out went Shardul Thakur, also an all-rounder of sorts. India turned to Suryakumar Yadav as an exclusive batter and Mohammed Shami as an exclusive bowler. The latter move paid off spectacularly.

Shami had played the two previous 50-over World Cups. But, even in England four years ago, he had been used only sparingly. Despite that, he finished with 14 wickets from four games, only behind Bumrah (18). Team balance had forced him to hog the bench this time until Pandya's unfortunate injury heralded his return. Shami took a wicket with his first ball of the tournament against New Zealand in Dharamsala and ended the game with five for 54, the first of three five-wicket hauls for him in seven matches. He would eventually finish with 24 wickets, the most by any bowler in the tournament.

India adjusted to the new normal superbly, Kohli shoring up the innings with three hundreds and the others expressing themselves without inhibition. Rohit continued to set the tempo, Gill came into his own after an understandably tepid start following illness, and Iyer and Rahul justified the faith placed in them as the rest of the teams were placed on notice. India meant business—*serious* business. They didn't just want to win; they were on a mission to crush their opponents. Everyone felt the heat—England, Sri Lanka, South Africa and lastly Netherlands. Unbeaten, India comfortably finished atop the league standings and then defeated New Zealand in a tall-scoring semifinal in Mumbai; Shami's seven for 57 killed off fledgling Kiwi hopes of hunting down their opponents' monumental 397 for four.

By this time, India had embarked on an enterprising exercise in the form of the fielding medal. The brainchild of fielding coach T. Dilip, it intended to celebrate the best fielder in each match, irrespective of the outcome. The initial plans were modest—just wrap the medal around the neck in the privacy of the dressing room—until the squad's media team came up with the grand design of making it a more visible and high-profile activity that involved past masters dropping in to award the medal. Novel methods were cooked up to announce the winner of the medal, including the name being flashed on the giant screen at the stadium. The fielding medal became such a hit that it gave the players added motivation to outdo themselves and their teammates.

Because these occasions were filmed and shared on social media, the outside world got to know what the team dynamics were. There was fun, there was banter, leg-pulling, genuine joy and kinship. This wasn't just a cricket team—a random collection of individuals. The sense of family that Rohit had instilled in that first chat in Thiruvananthapuram was affirmed with each passing day, helped along by the fact that all the members spent Diwali together with their families in tow. India were not just bossing the World Cup, they were positively enjoying themselves while doing so. The feeling that this was their time intensified with every passing day.

While India scythed through the draw, Australia snuck into the final by overcoming South Africa in a low-scoring thriller in the other semifinal in Kolkata. The Aussies had put India out of commission more than once in the World Cup, including eight years before in Melbourne. But Rohit's team believed they couldn't be denied this time. That belief stemmed from the kind of cricket they had played in the preceding seven weeks heading into the final.

Anti-climax

It was important to stay calm and relaxed before the final—or at least pretend to be that way—and for that too, the lead had to come from the captain. No matter what was going through his mind, Rohit was a picture of composure in the lengthy pre-final press conference, saying the right things and showing no signs of nerves or tension. His approachability and intent to facilitate the best dressing-room atmosphere apart, Rohit was also open to suggestions and therefore kept his wits about him ahead of the match.

Rohit and Pat Cummins, the Australian skipper, were to be involved in a trophy photo-shoot the day before the November 19 final. The shoot was at Adalaj Stepwell, an hour's drive from the hotel where the team was staying. People lined the streets to greet Rohit and a couple of members of the support team as their convoy made its way to the UNESCO heritage site, and the captain was astonished that so many would turn up just for a fleeting glimpse of the cavalcade.

It took him a while to comprehend that this was out of love for the team, that the vibes coming from the outside were positive and full of energy. When he stepped out of the vehicle at Adalaj Stepwell, the sea of people hit him like a shockwave. Gathering himself, he waved in every direction, sending those assembled into raptures. 'Class,' Rohit whispered as he sat on the steps. 'Just class.'

The next afternoon, Rohit began like a house on fire, like he had done all tournament long. Cummins's decision to field first took many by surprise. India had stacked up huge scores batting first and runs on the board had often proved decisive in a cup final. That belief was reinforced when Rohit got off to a frenetic start, racing away to 47 off just 30 deliveries. Cummins had turned to Glenn Maxwell as early as the eighth over and Rohit cashed in with a four in the off-spinner's first over, followed by a six and a four off successive deliveries in the next. With just three deliveries left in the Powerplay, Rohit went looking for a third straight boundary and sliced another attempted big hit down the ground. Travis Head was to deliver his first telling act of the final, running back from cover to hold a sensational catch.

That was a decisive moment in the contest.

From 76 for two in 9.4 overs, when Rohit was dismissed, India limped to 240 all out, dismissed off the last ball of their allotted 50 overs. It was runs on the board all right, but decidedly below par against a formidable Australian batting unit accustomed to turning up when it mattered the most. India knew they had left themselves 40 or 50 runs short and would have to play out of their skins to deny their nemesis. Despite a promising start with the ball, that wasn't to be. Head flayed them while making 137, Marnus Labuschagne weighed in with an unbeaten 58, and the Aussies raced home with six wickets in the bag and 42 deliveries to spare. The packed Narendra Modi Stadium went absolutely silent—the drop of a pin would have sounded like the clap of thunder.

After the customary shaking of hands and congratulating the winners, India trooped to the safety of their dressing room to vent their emotions. Tears flowed unchecked, not a dry eye in evidence. Rohit buried his face in his jersey, unwilling to expose his darkest moment to even his closest allies. There wasn't just disappointment; it was a devastating heartbreak. In that moment, India felt that they didn't deserve to lose—not after the way they had played in the ten previous matches.

Rohit's eyes were blood-red by the time of the presentation ceremony which followed, but he gathered himself and said all the right things even though the entire tournament

The Rise of the Hitman

flitted through his head like a tape on repeat. Prime Minister Narendra Modi dropped in to the Indian dressing room with a few words of consolation but most of it didn't register with the members of the team, who were in a trance.

Like a true leader, Rohit then took centre stage, telling his extended family that he was proud of them, that he wanted to applaud them for their commitment, excellence and professionalism. 'As a captain, there wasn't anything more I could have asked of you all. The passion, the desire, everyone playing their part so beautifully… I'd like to thank every one of you,' he told them. 'I know the result of the final will hurt, it won't be easy to get over it. Everyone will be down for a week or so, but once you get out of this stadium, try and put this behind you. There is a T20 World Cup not long from now and many in this room will be playing that tournament, so there is plenty to look forward to.'

It took a long time for the players and the support staff to gather their thoughts and finally make their way to the bus which would carry them to the hotel. On the way, they saw thousands of fans lining the streets to applaud them late into the night. It was a far cry from the past, when players' houses were stoned and effigies burned after India failed to advance beyond the first round of the 2007 World Cup in the Caribbean. That lifted their spirits briefly because the team realized that, while winning hearts wasn't the same as winning the cup, the joy they had provided their supporters was worth savouring, cherishing and being grateful for.

A dinner had been pre-organized at the hotel, where the families were also invited. It was supposed to have been a celebratory dinner. When Rohit finally walked into the room and saw his wife and daughter, he quickly approached them and lost himself in their embrace. As the group found solace in their respective families, the mood lifted slightly. On the outside, Rohit had played the statesman's role to perfection. But he was hurting inside. Immensely.

'After the 2023 World Cup final is the most gutted I've seen him,' Abhishek Nayar agrees. 'In my entire career, my entire friendship with him, as a colleague, a fellow player, a roomie, whatever, I haven't seen him as disappointed as I saw him that night. And let's be honest, he's gone through a lot. This one—this really hurt him. It was a very, very, *very* different Rohit who I met after the loss in the final. Even in the darkest times, he finds a way to crack a joke, he finds a way to keep it light. I don't know how he manages it, but he cracks a joke on his own predicament and has a hearty laugh usually. That night, only that night, it was all so different. We friends made an effort that night to actually be there with him, we tried not talking about it and stuff. But it was so evident to all of us that this guy was hurting like never before.'

It's an opinion seconded by Dinesh Karthik. 'It was not just the fact that India had lost the final,' Karthik observes, 'but also because of the manner in which they had played throughout the tournament that made the result unpalatable. To say that he was shattered will be an understatement. To him, it was all about winning the World Cup. The fact that it didn't happen, it took him some time to recover from that. On the way back to Mumbai after the final, he lost his phone, he lost his wallet, everything was gone. He was in a bad space for the next two or three days. I remember him telling me that he didn't even know where he was.

'Then he went off to London for a bit to clear his mind up a little. But the fact that the 50-over World Cup didn't have the ending that he had wanted, it didn't sit well with him at all.'

Cricket Must Go On: T20 World Cup, 2024

Packed calendars don't allow victories to sink in or defeats to be digested. In Rohit's case, a little over a month after the 19 November heartbreak, a two-Test series beckoned in South Africa, followed by a five-Test faceoff against England at home between January and March 2024. India salvaged a 1-1 draw from the former and then bounced back from an Ollie Pope-inflicted crippling loss in Hyderabad to crush England 4-1. Then came the IPL where, for the first time since 2013, Rohit did not lead Mumbai Indians. He had a terrific season personally, including making a second IPL century, but his team had a campaign to forget.

The leadership group at MI had bought Pandya back from Gujarat Titans as their new captain, their plans for the future not communicated to Rohit like they ought to have been perhaps. Pandya had led the Titans to the title on the franchise's debut in 2022 and to the final the following year, where a last-ball four from Jadeja muscled Chennai Super Kings to a popular fifth crown. His replacing Rohit at the helm of the MI set-up didn't go down well with fans. Pandya was unfairly booed at all venues, including at MI's home base—the Wankhede Stadium.

And there were whispers that his relationship with Rohit had soured beyond repair.

You wouldn't have guessed, seeing them in operation as captain and deputy at the T20 World Cup in the Americas in June. There was synergy, oneness and a unity of purpose; Rohit and Pandya were certainly not at cross-purposes and that was evident long before Rohit placed a spontaneous kiss on Pandya's cheek, moments after India had pulled the rug from South Africa's feet to snatch a final that was rapidly running away from them.

Unlike the 50-over World Cup, which he had to leave prematurely due to injury, Pandya was one of the driving forces of India's progress to the title by weighing in with influential displays throughout the tournament—most notably in the closing stages of the title clash when he picked up three wickets in his last two overs. Like seven months previously, but without the same chutzpah because they were shackled by terrible pitches at New York's Nassau County International Cricket Stadium, India bustled through the draw. Undefeated going into the Super Eights—they won their first three Group A fixtures before the final game against Canada was abandoned in Fort Lauderhill—they swept past Afghanistan and Bangladesh before old foes Australia lined up against them.

This was payback time.

India had defeated Australia in the respective opening league ties for both teams in the longer World Cup in Chennai but victory in Gros Islet came with greater ramifications. Afghanistan had already stunned Australia by then and if India could stack up their sixth successive win of the tournament, it would push the Aussies to the brink of elimination. Rohit wielded his willow like a scimitar, raining one crippling blow after another to breeze to 92 off just 41 deliveries. Eight sixes and seven fours cascaded off his punishing weapon, all his pent-up anger, remorse and disappointment finding positive release against the team that had crushed his long-cherished dream. India eventually won by 24 runs to storm into the semis, their delight doubled when Afghanistan edged out Bangladesh and sent Australia crashing from the competition.

All-conquering India's reward for their consistency was a shot in the last four against England, the defending champions who had swatted them aside by ten wickets in the corresponding clash a little over a year and a half ago in Adelaide. With Rohit taking charge again, India amassed 171 for seven on a dodgy pitch in Providence and then rode on the strength of their spinners to skittle Jos Buttler's holders for 103. This was as comprehensive a victory as any. A second final of a limited-overs World Cup in seven months—both times unbeaten reaching that stage—was colossal, but there was still some unfinished business.

Right?

The manner in which the final against South Africa was won and lost has been well chronicled, but as he pounded the turf in ecstasy after the last ball in Bridgetown, the wisdom of Rohit's words after the Ahmedabad loss became evident once again. Rohit aside, five members of this playing XI—Kohli, Suryakumar, Jadeja, Kuldeep and Bumrah—had played the 50-over final. For them, this victory would have been even sweeter—more all-encompassing, more fulfilling and more meaningful.

'When the 2024 World Cup happened, when they won this World Cup, we got on a video call that night,' Nayar recalls. 'When we were talking to Rohit, he was lying down, holding the trophy in his arms. He said, "*bhai, isko toh mai jaane doonga nahi;* I am not letting this go." It was like a young kid boasting about a massive achievement in a very fun-loving way. You could see the child in him come out with the trophy, with the happiness of having that trophy. It really mattered a lot to him, especially after the 2023 World Cup final, to go on and win this. Everyone was so happy that this had happened to him, because no matter what, it will be really hard for him for the rest of his life to reconcile to the fact that he had come so close and not got his hands on the (50-over) trophy.'

Karthik is of the view that the T20 World Cup was a mission for Rohit, a mission to set the record straight. 'The fact that he got an opportunity in the T20 World Cup, that reignited his fire. He had a journey that he knew he could become successful in.'

Vikram Rathour experienced the lowest of lows in Ahmedabad and the ultimate high in Bridgetown from the dressing room. 'Honestly, Rohit was somebody who was really keen to win a World Cup as a captain. He believed we had the team to achieve that. That 50-over World Cup, I believe we were by far the best team in the tournament—the way we played, the way we dominated, the kind of vibe we had in the group, in the team, it really felt like something special was going to happen. Until, unfortunately, we lost in the final.

'We wanted to bat with intent. We had enough depth in our batting. And we wanted to put the opposition under pressure and score as many runs as possible. For Rohit to be able to do that opening the batting, to go in there and play almost selflessly and not think too much about his personal performances, that is the kind of trend he set. The way the team responded to that—the kind of cricket we played during that World Cup—gave him even more conviction that this was the way to go.

'And he carried that into the T20 World Cup as well. We always had a solid batting group. But somewhere in white-ball cricket, that intent at times was missing sometimes. We felt that, especially so in T20 cricket. This was the World Cup where everything fell in place.'

12

A Match Made in Cricketing Heaven

A month before the start of the 2021 T20 World Cup in the United Arab Emirates, Virat Kohli announced that he would surrender the captaincy of the 20-over team at the conclusion of India's campaign to give himself the 'space to be fully ready to lead the Indian team in Test and ODI cricket.' This was on 16 September. By 31 October, India's World Cup was all but done following losses to Pakistan and New Zealand. They still had three league games left against Afghanistan, Scotland and Namibia—all of which they won—but that counted for little in the final analysis.

Kohli's abdication of the T20 throne didn't generate a huge stir. There would be no captaincy void—Rohit was seen as a natural successor. By then, not only had he led Mumbai Indians to five IPL titles, he had also stepped in for Kohli whenever the latter was not available, famously leading the team to the 20-over Nidahas Trophy success in Colombo in March 2018.

From Shastri to Dravid

The desert T20 World Cup would also be the swansong for Ravi Shastri, head coach since July 2017 after succeeding Anil Kumble in that role. During his four-year-long second stint with the national side—he had been the team director for two years before, from 2014 to 2016—Shastri had struck up a wonderful working relationship with Kohli.

A shrewd thinker and a top-class man-manager, Shastri had allowed Kohli to hog the limelight while working tirelessly behind the scenes in conjunction with his support group of first Sanjay Bangar and then Vikram Rathour as batting coaches, B. Arun as the bowling coach and R. Sridhar as the fielding coach.

Who would fill the Shastri-shaped breach? Rahul Dravid was seen as the obvious fit; he had spent four years—from 2015 to 2019—moulding the future of Indian cricket by coaching the India Under-19 and A squads, after which he took charge of the National Cricket Academy in Bengaluru. But he had a young family—two boys just about making their move in age-group cricket—and was initially reluctant to commit so much time away from home.

Sourav Ganguly, Dravid's long-time teammate and predecessor as India's captain, was the BCCI president at the time and somehow managed, along with his team, to convince his former deputy to come on board as the head coach. It was a massive coup that would change the dynamics of Indian cricket.

The deciding authorities were against splitting the white-ball captaincy. So, once Kohli stepped down as T20I skipper, they handed over the limited-overs leadership responsibilities entirely to Rohit while Kohli stayed on at the helm in the five-day game until abruptly announcing his resignation during the South Africa tour of January 2022.

By this time, Rohit was firmly entrenched in the Test XI as well. Therefore, the selectors conferred upon him the Test captaincy as well, making him the new all-format leader. But how would Rohit and Dravid—the man under whom he had made his international debut back in 2007—gel? On the face of it, they were fairly contrasting personalities—Rohit came across as laidback while Dravid was nothing if not serious.

Would they get on the same page?

Oh, they most certainly would.

Coach Dravid and Captain Rohit

It might have seemed like an unlikely match, but Rohit and Dravid forged a relationship for the ages, characterized by trust, openness, honesty and an unwavering commitment to the larger cause. They might not have known each other too well when they were thrown together as a leadership group, but by the end of Dravid's tenure in June 2024, they had become more than friends. Indeed, Dravid has acknowledged the role Rohit's phone call played after India's defeat to Australia in the final of the 50-over World Cup—at the time, his last assignment—in him agreeing to continue for seven more months in the hot seat.

Dravid's early memories of Rohit are vivid. 'Obviously, he came with a reputation. He was scoring a lot of runs in junior cricket in Mumbai and there was a lot of talk about Rohit Sharma.

The Rise of the Hitman

I remember seeing him in a Challenger Series tournament (in Chennai in October 2006 when Dravid, then the India captain, led India Blue and Rohit played for India Red). You could see he was really terrific, a special talent,' Dravid notes. 'He then came on the tour of Ireland when I was captain (in 2007), though we didn't play a lot together at the time. But in those early years, I kind of followed him—got to know him a little bit. He was really precocious and very shy. One thing I'd say about Rohit then was that he was not loud or in your face; a much quieter kind of kid, very shy, very respectful.

'But you could see he was a really special talent. In that Challengers, he didn't score many runs but it was obvious this boy had something slightly different from a lot of the other players. He was with the Test team in my last series (Australia, 2011–12) and by this time, he was certainly less shy and more comfortable than in 2007.'

Over time, Dravid got to know Rohit better, starting with when Dravid was roped in as consultant before the start of India's Test tour of England in 2014. 'I spent a week in England and had a few conversations with Rohit, talking to him about his batting and his technique. The transformation was visible. By then, he was a much more established One-Day player still trying to find his feet in Test match cricket. And in the lead-up to my coaching stint, I met him at the NCA (where Dravid was the head at the time) when he was injured and we had a few conversations around the team—what his philosophies were, how he saw the game. When I was still deciding about the coaching thing—by then, Virat had announced his resignation and Rohit was going to take over the white-ball role—we had a few chats around the direction of the team and where it was, just to get a sense and gauge whether he would be comfortable with me coming on board.

'He'd come home once or twice previously for a meal with Ajinkya (Rahane) and so we had some level of relationship. But in the time that we spent together as coach and captain, we became a lot closer. You just have so many conversations, you make so many decisions together, conversations about other people, messages to be communicated to people on the decisions made, giving people a lot of clarity… We both spent time investing in the relationship. I've always found him very generous; he's got a great humility about him, a great respect. However busy he's been, he's always had time for me or the team, he's been very invested in the whole process.'

Dravid led India very successfully—the 2007 50-over World Cup debacle notwithstanding—for two years. Therefore, he has had a first-hand taste of what an Indian captain goes through over an extended period of time. 'Sometimes, it can get tough as a captain, because there's so many things,' he elaborates. 'You have to look after your own performances. Sometimes, things outside the field—whether it's tactical, whether it's meetings, whether it's discussions—they can weigh you down. But I've always found him very, very invested in that process and that was a very reassuring thing for me, because if you wanted to discuss stuff with him, you knew he was going to give it his time. He was going to think about it, he wasn't just going to be flippant about it. Even if, at times, it was tough or irritating for him, he never let it show. He was very committed in understanding that his role was very important—whether it was being part of team meetings, understanding the strategy, understanding thinking, sitting with the analyst. He was very good with that.'

An intense individual who throws himself whole-heartedly into every task he undertakes, Dravid admits that even he was awestruck by Rohit's involvement in the cause. 'A lot of times, I'd tell him that he didn't really need to come for this, we're just sitting down as coaches and having a meeting and discussing, but he'd say he wanted to be a part of that. He's very good at compartmentalizing his life. He's very good with his family, he's a very strong family man—very much devoted to his family, his wife, his kid—and he's really brilliant with them. But he's also able to move on from that and be completely here when it's required to be here. That's not an easy trait to have; things can sometimes spill over but he's been very good with that and Ritika has really supported him very well in that.

'The team sees that level of involvement in, commitment to and interest in the process—in what we're doing—and that helps him with the boys because then the boys readily relate to him. They understand that he's putting in a lot of effort and time. He's sitting in on bowling meetings, he's not just coming and telling them a strategy without doing the work himself. He's also quite unflappable as a person, quite relaxed. Like anyone, I'm sure he gets tense and gets quite nervous about things. But he is quite good with understanding and being balanced about the results. Obviously, there's a lot riding on some of these wins and losses, and especially in the lead-up to ICC tournaments, there was always this thing of "we haven't won an ICC tournament for so long". It almost felt like Rohit had been given the captaincy so that we could win an ICC tournament because he had won the IPL so many times. Maybe he did feel that pressure to some extent—a little bit of pressure—mainly during those big tournaments.

'That pressure of expectation, everyone feels it; it's hard not to feel it. Especially because of the disappointments a lot of them had gone through, coming so close so many times over the last so many years, maybe that desperation was there. But again, he was very good at not allowing that to reflect on the outside. The team probably never saw it, which was very good.'

Again, through experience, Dravid knows better than most that it's impossible for a captain to be friends with everyone. Yet, Rohit seems to have managed that quite effortlessly with most of his colleagues, if not all. 'That's because he is quite direct about things,' Dravid says without pause. 'And he has time for people, right? As a captain, you are taking tough decisions all the time. You're picking and dropping people, batting orders. To still be able to maintain that level of friendship and relationship is (a) credit to him. A large part of that is because of his personality. He puts himself out there; he's quite open in the sense that he's willing to explain things to people, to communicate the reason behind the decision-making. Sometimes I would tell him, "Hey, don't worry, I'll do it," and he'd say, "No, no, no, it's okay, I'll do it. I need to do it to that person." I was amazed that he was happy to have those difficult conversations with people. Maybe that's endeared him to a lot of the boys. He's been able to maintain that distance as well as be one among the boys. He's taken the trouble to have the time in their relationships. He's always there when people have reached out to him.'

By the time he left the Indian coaching set-up, Dravid had firmed up an ever-lasting relationship with Rohit as well as his family—wife Ritika and daughter Samaira—but he is honest in stating that he had no idea how this relationship would evolve when they were thrown together into the deep end in early 2022. 'You don't know how things will unfold when you get into any relationship, right? Even from before I became the coach, I've really been fond of Rohit. I really enjoyed the way he batted. I have told him so many times that watching him play the pull shot was one of the joys of my coaching stint; my last ten years really, but especially when I was coaching him. Watching him play that pull shot has been so much fun.

'But you never know, right?' Dravid says again. 'These things are tricky relationships. But I'm glad it really worked out. I admire his role and what he's done for Indian cricket, what a player he's been. But I also think we both respected each other. We respected each other's space, but I knew that he would always back me when things got tough. I'd like to believe that he too felt the same. I told him early on that I'll support him and back any team that he puts on the park. But we need to discuss it, have conversations around it. The one good thing was that we would thrash out issues and come up with a solution if we didn't necessarily agree on certain things, and when we walked out of the room, we were very clear that the decision was both our decisions.'

When Dravid's tenure ended, Ritika said in a social media post that more than anyone else, Samaira would miss his company. Dravid also cherishes his interactions with Rohit's daughter. 'I'm very fond of his daughter, and his wife's a lovely girl as well. We spent so much time together; you do get (a) little close. When Rohit and I started our journey, it was a relationship built on fondness to start off with from my side, then just deep respect for the work that he's doing. I was very appreciative of the time he spent, his commitment to Indian cricket, his commitment to the team, which is what I wanted as a coach. I'm sure there are things he liked about what I did, so it kind of seemed to work quite well.'

One common perception is that it was the ten-wicket loss to England in Adelaide in the semifinal of the 2022 T20 World Cup that compelled India to change their brand of cricket. 'People use that semifinal as a changing point but honestly, in our first meetings itself, we were on the same page that we needed to change the way we were playing T20 cricket,' Dravid stresses. 'If you notice our scores from, say, the UAE World Cup to the T20 World Cup in Australia, you'd see a marked difference. The wheels had started to turn well before that semifinal loss.

'That England loss was a disappointment; perhaps the conditions suited England more. That kind of got flipped when we played them in Guyana (in the 2024 T20 World Cup semifinal) and we destroyed them when the conditions favoured us slightly more. But we were moving in that direction (of aggressive batting) well before that (Australia) World Cup. And we continued that into the 50-over World Cup—Rohit led that beautifully.'

Dravid is all praise for the way Rohit chose to set the tone. 'Once we recognized that was the way, he took it upon himself to try and play a more attacking, more positive brand of cricket—take the game on, move the game forward, lead by example,' he emphasizes. 'At times, I might have felt maybe he's batting so well that he should hold back or look to be a little bit more conservative. But we all realized that him setting the tone meant it would inspire the others. He kept playing that way and forced other people to come along with him because he was the guy leading from the front, right? And as an opener, he said, I need to do it even more because of the first ten overs. That really showed in that 50-over World Cup—the kind of scores we were able to put up, the way we played. Of course, it was a disappointment, losing the final after playing ten great games. But nothing changed even after that. We knew we needed to do the same things, keep repeating the same things, and hopefully the luck would change, and that's exactly what happened.'

Rohit is the master of big scores in white-ball cricket. He has three ODI double hundreds and a highest score of 264; in T20Is, he boasts five centuries. Dravid acknowledges the effort that has gone behind Rohit not bothering about personal milestones and instead concentrating solely on getting the team off to a furious start. 'It requires a lot of selflessness because there's a lot of easy runs to be scored at times in One-Day cricket—50-over cricket with two new balls, once you get past those initial phases, actually there's a lot of easy runs to be scored in the middle overs with the extra fielder in the ring. But it's not so much about the easy runs now because teams are scoring much faster. You need to score them at a much quicker rate now to be able to be competitive.

'He could easily have backed down and played a little

bit slower and no one would have said too much because it's not that he was ever a slow player. But he wanted to make a statement, set a benchmark. He wanted to keep that tempo going and that ensured that other people were forced to keep the tempo going; he was able to drag people along with him. You could say it's a lot easier when you're established, you're a big player, you've already got a great record behind you. But it's also very selfless because you know you've left those easy runs on the ground in trying to make a statement and be very aggressive.'

The 50-over World Cup campaign that Dravid alludes to was marked by breathtaking cricket from India. Till they lost to Australia in the final, India played a brand of cricket that captivated the whole world. They won, yes, but they also won magnificently, entertaining, enthralling and driving their millions of fans to the throes of ecstasy. Rohit was the engine room in every sense of the term, and when India came second best to Australia in the final in Ahmedabad, it was as if his world had collapsed around him.

Dravid was with Rohit in the dressing room minutes after that shattering loss and you can sense that even ten months on, the former head coach hasn't fully come to terms with it yet. 'Oh, he was disappointed,' Dravid says of Rohit. 'There was a huge amount of disappointment because we played really well throughout the tournament. One of the things we were very good at was in preparing—the process and planning. We'd done all of that and it almost felt like everything was coming together because it was quite challenging. Leading into the World Cup, there were a lot of injury concerns. We had to manage injuries. We had to manage players. There's incredible workload management. Sometimes, you have to sacrifice results to manage workloads, and we got to a point where we were saying, "Okay, what's more important is managing players rather than worrying about wins and losses."

'It's not easy in a country like India because people keep judging you all the time on every win and loss. It takes character to say, "I'm not really worried about the results, I'm focused on something larger in the future. But I'm also focused on the players, having value for the players and their well-being." As much as it is about the team, the players are also human beings. But to adopt that philosophy, both people (the captain and the coach) have to agree on that because in the end the record is going to show against his name, right?'

'That's why he was so disappointed following the loss in the final after that terrific run until then. He was quite hurt,' Dravid reveals, 'and that's probably why he wanted to have another crack at another ICC tournament. In some ways, I think if we had won that game in Ahmedabad, I'm not really sure—I don't know for certain—whether he would have played in the next T20 World Cup or he would have asked me to continue. But it's just that hurt of... I think both of us felt there was some unfinished business. We'd done a lot of good work and I think both of us felt we wanted to have one more crack at it. I'm glad he did, you know, it was just terrific.'

You can see just how much winning the T20 World Cup in the Caribbean means to Dravid, but he is quick to deflect the joy elsewhere. 'I just felt happy for him, he deserved it,' he adds emotionally. 'The fact that he was able to win an ICC trophy as a captain was truly well deserved for him. Between the two T20 World Cups, he played three games for India in the 20-over format because the focus was on the 50-over World Cup. We were always prioritizing things. It was such a busy calendar, particularly for the guys who were playing all three formats. Either it's the World Test Championship, it's the 50-over World Cup, or it's this. That was one of the biggest challenges, prioritizing, and he was very good at understanding that. We needed to ensure that we had our players rested and in good condition for the best series. I'm glad he just came in and it all worked out together.'

By the time of the T20 World Cup in the Caribbean, Rohit wasn't even captaining his IPL team anymore. 'And then to win the World Cup for India…' Dravid trails off. 'In some ways, there was a level of destiny to that.'

Dravid deconstructs Rohit's analytical side of captaincy. 'Tactically, he's really good. It's one of the things I've seen him grow as. The fact that he's captained in so many games, high-pressure games, obviously helps. Just go back to that World Cup final in Bridgetown, 30 runs needed by South Africa off 30 balls. He's been in those situations so many times—sometimes winning, sometimes losing—but the fact that he had been in those situations before allowed him to remain calm. If you see the way he captained in those five overs, it was brilliant captaincy.'

Falling back on his famed observational skills, he continues, almost in a trance, 'You know, Rohit was just so calm; bringing (Jasprit) Bumrah back at the right time; cutting the singles at the right time; giving a single at the right time to (Keshav) Maharaj; ensuring that Maharaj got on strike in the next over and played three dot balls against Arshdeep (Singh); all of these are small things. They're very subtle things—like having the right guy in the right place at the boundary. There was a level of calmness in a situation that seemed lost. That frustration could have come in, saying, "Here we go again, this is happening again to us." But the calmness he showed in those last 30 balls is a reflection of how much he has grown tactically and otherwise as a captain. For me, it was all encompassed in those 30 balls.

'The way he led, the way he stayed calm through all that. The way he stayed balanced through that. That shows you how much experience matters in captaincy and leadership. By being calm and being relaxed and making the right calls, you might not win every time. But it gives you a chance,' Dravid reasons. 'Right through, tactically too, he has been very good, very simple with his tactics. Like I said, he invests a lot of time to understand tactics and plans; he takes the time to work with bowlers. But he is also good at going with his gut. There were moments sometimes, even in Test cricket, when we'd wonder in the dugout why he was bringing a particular bowler on. It is not always that the change works, but you just feel that there is a thought process to it, not just a whim.

'One of his other standout features is that he doesn't get very emotional about things. He is very practical, very good at looking at a game and reading a game really well. And for all that, he's still a fun guy. He is able to find that balance. He is, like I said, very good at compartmentalizing things. He's very good at having fun with the guys and chilling out and letting his hair down when it is required, and being with his family when it is required. But he is also very good at switching on and stuff.'

As he casts a surreptitious glance at his watch, Dravid is game for one more Rohit narration. 'You remember that Test we lost to England in Hyderabad this January (2024), right? It was really disappointing to lose that game after being 190 runs ahead. We knew they were going to sweep and reverse sweep us. But when Ollie Pope played that innings (196) and swept and reverse swept to *that* extent, there was a little bit of stress and a worry in the group that "Man, if these guys keep playing like this, then what are we going to do next?"

'At the end of that game, Rohit said, "Let's all go out, let's just meet for a drink." It ended up becoming me, him, and the coaches and Ashwin. I remember him being so calm about it. He said, "That guy is not going to be able to play another innings like that again. No chance, man. That's ridiculous." I was like, I hope he is right. But I walked away from that evening feeling really reassured that this guy is disappointed with this loss, yes, but he knows what the way forward is. He understands that this is a one-off freaky thing but we're still on the right path.

'By then, we had lost K.L. Rahul and (Ravindra) Jadeja for the next Test in Visakhapatnam. Virat Kohli wasn't there. We had just lost a Test we should have won. It would have been easy for a captain to be down, to blame it on external elements, to maybe moan a bit, but I loved the way he was so calm about it—"Let's have a drink. Let's relax. Let's just chill."'

End result? India won the next four Tests.

Just chill.

13

The Man behind the 'Hitman'

Rohit Sharma is many things—a fabulous batter, an astute captain, and a warm, kind and generous human being who is fiercely loyal. Despite the giant strides he has taken as a cricketer, despite the fame, name, money and celebrity status that is inevitable when one becomes a cricketing superstar in India, he is still firmly grounded, not losing sight of his humble beginnings and grateful for whatever has come his way since he made it big with the national team.

His childhood friends remain his friends even today. The circle has expanded—as it invariably does when one moves ahead in life and interacts with more people—but the band of brothers with whom he bonded when he was just Rohit, not the Hitman, is still intact. With them, Rohit is at his witty and natural best, unafraid of being judged and compartmentalized. However, even otherwise, he is extremely comfortable in his own skin.

An inevitable fallout of the climb up the rungs of the social ladder is a dramatic change in personality. Sometimes, people are so caught up with the riches and attention coming their way that they are unrecognizable from what they were in the past. In Rohit's case, there is no such danger. He still is the same earthy and relatable human being as before, which is something that has endeared him to the people with whom he has interacted over the years.

V.V.S. Laxman has tracked his progress for more than a decade and a half, as a teammate, commentator, analyst and head of the National Cricket Academy—apart from briefly stepping in as the coach when Rahul Dravid was unavailable.

'What I remembered of Rohit in 2008 (during the IPL when the two were with Deccan Chargers) was that he used to hang out with his friends. And what I saw in the Asia Cup, in the changing room, was the same,' Laxman notes. 'His language didn't change, the way he was bantering with his friends didn't change. He was a very normal guy. To me, that was great to see. Irrespective of whether he was the captain or not, irrespective of whether he had become a senior player or not, the slang, the way he speaks, that didn't change.

'There was no affectation, no put-on or show. He didn't think that he had to do things differently just because he was the captain of the Indian team, and that was brilliant. Sometimes, when you play a lot of international cricket, you tend to become a little circumspect even in a private setting; you try to be a little careful about what you are talking, where you are talking, to whom you are talking. But with Rohit, that's not the case. At a certain level, there is no filter, if I may say so. He will say things as he sees them, as he feels them.'

Laxman still remembers with great fondness those four

The Rise of the Hitman

days in the Indian dressing room in Dubai during the T20 Asia Cup in 2022. 'It was just fantastic watching him go about his business. Especially with his peers, he was very open. He was not worried about what people might think about the way he talks. That's why he was very natural within the group and everyone was comfortable with him. You know how it can occasionally be—you might be having an uninhibited conversation within a group and then someone else walks in and you go all quiet suddenly. Rohit has never been like that. He has nothing to hide, he has no malice. There are no two sides to him; he is what he appears to be."

Abhishek Nayar, who became one of India's assistant coaches in 2024, has been in Rohit's tight circle of friends for a long, long time and knows him as well as anyone else. He offers a more nuanced perspective of Rohit's journey. 'What I can tell you is—and I think this is really crucial—that a lot of people have said that Rohit hasn't changed a lot from what he was when he was younger. If anything, I'd say there is always a change, but it's (a) change for the good.

'You can see that his robust nature of saying what he wants, he's brought a bit of culture to it, and he's brought a bit of class to it as well. But he's not lost his unique, funny and always light-natured self. Even today, he's retained that miraculously, with everything that he's gone through and everything that he's evolved into.

'He's not changed with regard to how much fun he still has in the small little things in life—just sitting with friends and having a conversation and talking about the silliest things and laughing. It tells you that even today, the smallest things make him happy and the closest friends that he had then are still his closest friends. Even that hasn't changed—and it changes a lot of players, you know. People evolve and how they carry themselves evolve. I think with Rohit, that evolution has been great.'

His closest friends form a group of about half a dozen people, most—but not all—of whom are cricketers. But it is not only in this group that two-way banter flows. Rohit has the uncanny knack of putting even the youngest member in his various teams at ease, which separates him from many others. 'One of the things he loves the most is banter,' Nayar chuckles. 'He loves it, so he encourages it. And you know, it's not one-way banter. With a lot of people, it is one-way. They say stuff and they laugh but then when the joke is on them, they aren't amused. With Rohit, it's completely different. He'll say something and then it's an open door. You'll say something back and he'll laugh at himself. That's a rare gift.

'It's so funny. He's a terrific character, he won't ever make you feel "Oh, what have I done? I have said something to Rohit Sharma" type of thing ever, which is why the youngsters also find it very easy to just crack a joke. I think he lets it happen because he enjoys it himself.'

Dinesh Karthik is another close friend, their relationship going back to 2007 and Rohit's international debut. 'In all ways, I have inadvertently caused him a lot of trouble, which ended up being great,' Karthik laughs uproariously, taking credit for his excellent middle-order run in ODIs which, he claims, forced Mahendra Singh Dhoni to promote Rohit to the opener's slot. 'And without a doubt, ahead of the 2022

(T20) World Cup (in Australia), he supported me, he wanted me in the team. We've always had banter and a lot of affection for each other. He's someone I can rely on, no matter what happens.'

Karthik echoes Nayar's sentiments when he says, 'He's very helpful. He still looks out for a lot of his close friends. His friends back in the day are still his close friends and I value that a lot. He takes care of them and does whatever is required for them to live a happy life. He's a very chill person. But he is also a very family-oriented guy. Even today, before going on a tour, he will go to Borivali to see his mom and dad.'

Rohit is a people person who thinks nothing of stopping his car in the middle of a bustling Mumbai street because a fan wants him to wish her on her birthday and a selfie to mark the occasion. He is also a philanthropist, although that's something he'd rather keep under wraps because he doesn't do it for public attention.

'What I will tell you is that he has a big heart,' Nayar says. 'This was around 2009 or 2010, when one of our colleagues— he wasn't even a friend but a colleague, someone who was seven-eight years older than us—was going through a family issue and didn't have a place to stay. I remember us going up to Rohit and saying, "You live in Bandra in a big three-bedroom apartment and you're alone. Would you mind helping him out till he can sort himself out and find a place to stay?" Believe it or not, that guy stayed with Rohit for two years! He figured himself out, figured his life out. He stayed with him, he ate with him; he was like a member of Rohit's family.

'This is just a small example of who Rohit Sharma

actually is. A lot of people don't know that. For him, giving away something or helping someone comes naturally.'

Nayar credits Ritika with not just bringing stability and calmness to his life but also for polishing the rough edges. 'Ritika has had a very positive impact on Rohit's life. In a very funny way, I say in culturing him outside of it, from outside of the game, in how he carried himself. But he still finds ways to let loose every now and then, when you see the funny Rohit outside of it,' he guffaws. 'Ritika has been the greatest impact in Rohit's life in a lot of ways. She brought not only a lot of stability, but also a direction for him in life and took away a lot of his headaches, things that he's not very good at.

'She is instrumental in completing his journey as a sportsperson wherein he had the support to go out and just play the sport without worrying about any other thing, which is anyway not his forte. In terms of his own individual development as a cricketer, he's always been supremely talented, he's always been a person who's taken disappointments head-on. When I say taking disappointments head-on, Rohit has only one way of overcoming disappointment and that is going back and digging in, whether that be in practice, whether that be with his training, whether that be going into a zone with his diet. For him, it's plain and simple—if things don't work out, he goes back and gets into his zone and it's been something he's been able to do over and over again, which is amazing.'

Over the years, because of their respective schedules, Rohit and Nayar haven't been able to work together a lot from a cricketing standpoint, but that changed after their coming together within the Indian team's leadership set-up.

The Rise of the Hitman

In 2024, Rohit had a layoff of sorts between the end of the T20 World Cup on 29 June and the start of the international home season in Chennai on 19 September. 'After a really long time—when we both had been busy in different things—we were able to spend plenty of time together. And the amount of sacrifices he's made in regard to his nutrition, in regard to how disciplined he's with his food, in regard to training two sessions a day, every single day, to prolong his career—that epitomized everything that Rohit is. We did that in 2011 (after the World Cup disappointment), we did that in 2016, and then to see him again in 2024, going through the grind, that just told me that not a lot has changed.

'He knows when to push himself and that's always been part of his journey as a cricketer. His evolution has been strange because if you ask his close friends and you ask us, that period from 2009 to 2011—when there were lots of questions asked of Rohit Sharma and a lot of things were said, it's amazing how he's overcome all of that without too much cribbing, without too much worrying about what everyone said—to today being an iconic cricketer worldwide, it's an amazing transformation, without losing any part of himself, which is his greatest achievement.'

Rohit's down-to-earth behaviour when it comes to his inner circle is something Nayar treasures. 'Any of us can call him at any time and he will respect that,' he reveals. 'He wouldn't want to feel entitled in front of his friends or feel like he's someone big or a *celebrity*. He still has that normalcy in his life. That's not something he tries to show people; it's just something he is. It's one thing him saying it, and it's another thing, people around him feeling it. Me or all his close friends, we can still joke with him, say what we want to and get away with it without worrying about who we are saying it to. For us, it's still talking to the same old Rohit. These are all very rare qualities you have in an individual. I believe a lot of people have rare qualities but to not let go of them in a successful career, that is the hallmark of a person like Rohit. He's not let go of all these things that make him so lovable and endearing to everyone.'

Like Nayar, Karthik too is reluctant to talk much about Rohit's involvement with charity, though he says that when a cause resonates with him, he plunges into it wholeheartedly. 'I know he did a campaign with Adidas for, I think, the "don't use plastic" campaign. How plastic affects the environment. I know that his daughter (Samaira) really loves the sea and that's why they keep going to the Maldives because they enjoy it as a family. And that's when he started developing a fondness for the ocean and everything that's under it.

'So, he promoted this campaign about not throwing plastic as waste in the ocean. It's something he was very fierce about. I remember he had a shoe made where the "save the ocean" message and campaign was very clear. He was very serious about it.'

Yuvraj Singh has plenty of Rohit stories, including this gem. 'I was once bowling to (Andrew) Flintoff during a game against England and he hit me back over my head,' Yuvraj manages to narrate amidst fits of uproarious laughter. 'Gautam (Gambhir) ran to his right from long-off and dived and stopped the ball, then threw it towards (Suresh) Raina, who was converging from long-on. The ball sailed over Raina's head and landed outside the boundary. The umpire signalled a four when Rohit came and told me it should have been a six. "It landed on the full outside the rope," he kept insisting! I pointed out that it had hit the turf before Gautam stopped it, but he would have none of it, said it was a six without doubt. I am just glad he didn't take up umpiring!

'He's otherwise also a very funny guy, very humble and very sweet. And he forgets everything—I am telling you, *everything*. He only remembers that his name is Rohit Sharma! And he remembers how to bat, thank God for that. I'd kept telling him that Ritika was the right girl to marry. He also remembers that. He seldom listened to my advice, if that's the word, but I am glad the one thing that he paid heed to, which is marrying Ritika, has made his life better.

'He's one person who hasn't changed as a human being. Whether he's the captain or not, whether he's in the team or out of it, whether he's scoring hundreds or zeroes, he's never changed as a person,' Yuvraj says. 'That's what I love about him. And that's what everyone will tell you—from his *paanwallah* to his old friends from Borivali.'

Karthik and Nayar have both had a first-hand taste of the highs and lows that Rohit experienced. Apart from the bitter disappointment of the loss in the 2023 World Cup final, it is his calmness and ability to remain unfazed in the most trying of circumstances that appeals to them the most.

'It's something that he was innately born with. He used to have a lot of fun off the field—do whatever. But when it came to his cricket, he was always serious,' Karthik observes. 'He came across as someone who could be seen to be lazy because of the way he played. But by no means was he lazy. He used to work as hard as anybody. He had his own way of doing things. And he was very serious about his batting and what his vision was. After he became a leader, he was clear about how he wanted to proceed with the team that he handled.

'He was tactically sound; he understood the game well. And most importantly, his greatest strength is the fact that he connects with people off the field. People think his cover drive or his pull shot is one of his greater strengths. But his greatest strength is this ability to bounce back from setbacks. And he's had plenty, be it injuries, be it the way he's been treated in terms of being part of a team, be it being dropped for the 2011 World Cup. Each time, he bounced back. His resilience came through and *that* is his greatest strength.'

Rohit is a riot in the changing room and he is pretty much the same on the field, as evidenced by his hilarious one-liners that are caught by the stump microphone. He lets his colleagues know exactly what he is thinking in wonderfully colourful language and—despite its un-parliamentary parlance—the complete absence of malice compels people to roll over in laughter.

'What he was in 2007 is exactly what he is today in 2024 as well. It's amazing, all the accolades he's got...' Karthik's wonderment is obvious. 'Very relaxed, chilled out. He still speaks the same way. He can speak in a very, very polished manner. At the same time, he also talks like how only guys can speak amongst friends.'

Dhawal Kulkarni, the former India and Mumbai paceman,

has spent many a riotous evening with Rohit, either on tours or at the latter's home. Their careers almost overlapped, although Rohit is a year and a half older. 'Mumbai cricket, really, is the origin of our friendship,' Kulkarni chuckles. 'We played for the same college (Rizvi College) and then the state side. Right from the beginning, he was very down to earth, humble and he had that friendly vibe, which made him easy to approach. He continues to be that way even 17–18 years later, which is awesome.

'He has always been someone who loves spending time with friends. When we were playing for college together, we were a group of friends—some from outside cricket as well—who'd forever hang together. We made a lot of memories outside of cricket, be it small trips outside Mumbai, maybe a get-together of sorts, a dinner perhaps. He was the one who drove those gatherings.'

Even today, Rohit isn't averse to enjoying *vada paav* from a regular stall in Worli. For all his socially upward climb, he remains aware of his roots and humble beginnings.

Kulkarni speaks of a certain fondness Rohit had for his two-wheeler during his early days in representative cricket. 'He loved riding bikes, he had this sports bike which he used to ride from his Borivali residence to the Wankhede Stadium,' Kulkarni remembers. 'He used to park it at the ground and after the game, he'd ride it over and over again on Marine Drive. We'd go for dinner to the stadium restaurant or to his place where he used to live before, in Bandra.

'When we had a break from cricket, many of us would practically live there and have great fun. We used to play

PlayStation till late in the night; Rohit was very competitive and hated losing. And when I say late in the night, I mean we'd start playing around 9.30 p.m. and end up playing till 6.00 or 7.00 in the morning. Just normal, you know!'

As Yuvraj alluded to earlier, Rohit is also famously and hilariously forgetful—*Ghajini*, the character Aamir Khan played in the film of the same name, has often been associated with him. And while he affects annoyance at the reference, you can see that it amuses him. On Kapil Sharma's comedy show, Shivam Dube and Suryakumar Yadav wasted no time in reflecting on Rohit's 'amnesia', with the skipper himself an interested listener. Dube spoke of how Rohit often forgot his teammates' names at the toss. 'Not just names, he even forgets to take the coin when he goes out for the toss,' Suryakumar quipped. Rohit was the first to burst out laughing, reiterating Nayar's assertion that he is as good at being at the receiving end of banter as dishing it out. The Dube-Suryakumar episode was another illustration of the erosion of the class divide which was once the bane of Indian cricket, where juniors were expected to be subservient to seniors and where such reverse leg-pulling was viewed with horrified indignation.

'He has forgotten his laptop, his iPad at the airport,' Kulkarni laughs. 'And he didn't mind us having a laugh at his expense. Over the years, he has matured as an individual. But he has always been a light-hearted guy who likes to have fun, who is always cracking jokes.'

Forgetfulness hasn't been a Rohit ally all the way through, Parthiv Patel insists. 'When I was in Mumbai Indians (2015–17), I didn't notice any of it. But maybe I was in my own world and it escaped me,' he says. Perhaps it did escape Parthiv, because not long after his marriage to Ritika (13 December 2015), Rohit went into panic mode when he realized that he had left his wedding ring in his hotel room and boarded the team bus headed for the airport.

Rohit himself recalled that incident during a conversation with Gaurav Kapur on the latter's *Breakfast with Champions* show. 'I was recently married and I wasn't in the habit of wearing a ring. So whenever I went to sleep, I'd take the ring off,' said Rohit, who confessed to being notoriously late to get to the team bus, either for a match or to go to the airport. He'd urge one or more of his teammates to wake him up in good time, but that day no one knocked on his door and by the time he got up, it was also time for the bus to leave. In his rush, Rohit completely forgot about the wedding ring until he saw Umesh Yadav walk past him in the bus, sporting his own wedding ring.

'I took Bhajju *pa* (Harbhajan Singh) aside and quietly told him to request a person he knew at the hotel to bring the ring to the airport,' Rohit revealed. He tried to keep the episode as quiet as possible in order to avoid any further embarrassment, but to his great consternation, Virat Kohli informed the entire team of what had transpired, Rohit added with a chuckle.

Another in a series of such unforgettable incidents unfolded at the toss during a One-Day International against New Zealand in Raipur in January 2023. Tom Latham, the Kiwi skipper, called wrong and match referee Javagal Srinath informed Rohit that he had won the toss. For a good 15 seconds—no exaggeration, it's freely available to view on YouTube—Rohit blanked out, unable to recall the pre-decided choice he was supposed to make if he happened to win the toss. Latham and Srinath could hardly control themselves when Rohit finally had his Eureka moment and said, 'We'll bowl first.' His relieved laughter at having found the answer to the trickiest question in the exam paper was quintessentially Rohit, one of the primary reasons why he is beloved by so many.

14

A Lasting Legacy

Within four months of masterminding one of Indian cricket's greatest triumphs, Rohit oversaw the most debilitating of defeats, a 0–3 Test series loss to New Zealand on home turf. India had won every one of the preceding 18 series over a 12-year period in their backyard and were expected to put it past the Kiwis, just like they had done against Bangladesh a fortnight ago. But they came seriously unstuck, unable to counter the left-arm spin of Mitchell Santner and Ajaz Patel in successive games on turning tracks, after erroneously opting to bat first on a seaming surface in Bengaluru during the first Test.

Rohit had a series to forget as batter and leader and immediately accepted responsibility—a rarity in an era where the convenient option is to point fingers elsewhere. Some termed it as a 'PR exercise', but that is more reflective of a cynical mindset than any subterfuge on the Indian captain's part.

It will be churlish to measure Rohit against the New Zealand debacle alone, however dispiriting it might have been. His own poor form extended to Australia, where he sat out the final Test in Sydney, convinced that on current form he didn't merit a place in the best Indian XI. He took charge at a difficult time, following the breakdown of relations between Virat Kohli and the Board of Control for Cricket in India, and formed a spectacular association with Rahul Dravid, his first international captain whose contributions as head coach in the growth of Rohit as an individual and a leader-cum-batter can't be exaggerated.

One of Rohit's more significant contributions is in forcing his colleagues to focus beyond individual accomplishments. In the past, millions of fans went home happy as long as their heroes did well—even if their team ended up losing. Perhaps subconsciously that spawned an era of concentrating on milestones, with more than greater significance attached to a century or a five-wicket haul. Rohit ensured that such individual milestones didn't come at the expense of the team.

Because he himself didn't slow down while approaching a fifty or a hundred, those around him experienced first-hand the detached attachment the captain was espousing. It was always team first; more than once, Rohit has proclaimed that success or failure is a collective outcome, not because of one or two individuals. Rohit is not the first Indian captain to emphasize the strength of the collective, but few others have been able to get their colleagues to uncomplainingly buy into the concept as comprehensively as the Mumbaikar.

V.V.S. Laxman is nothing if not impressed by what Rohit has been able to achieve in his relatively short stint as the Indian captain. 'He has retired (internationally) from one format (T20s), he is playing in other formats,' Laxman points out.

The Rise of the Hitman

'But he has cemented his legacy, he has got the results. He has got a World Cup title. He has taken the team to another World Cup final. Will he go down as one of the more influential captains in Indian cricket? Definitely.

'Even though he has not captained India a lot—what's it been, two and a half years?—he has shown in that time how and what a team can do as a unit. Everyone has contributed to victories during this period. One of the things that has stood out for me is how single-mindedly Rohit stuck to game plans. Sometimes, when you decide on a style of play, then you are hesitant if the results don't go your way while following that style and therefore players can sometimes not toe the line. But Rohit backed them and allowed them to execute those plans. That for me is a big legacy he will leave behind—creating an environment where it's calm, where everyone can trust the leader and where no one has that fear of failure.'

Laxman played for India under several captains and is quick to point out that his observations on Rohit are no reflection on the leaders under whom he went to battle. 'Trust in the leader is very important and there is no one within the Indian set-up who does not trust Rohit,' Laxman insists. 'Everyone can vouch for that. As a leader, you obviously disappoint some players with your choices, with your decisions. But everyone knows that none of it is personal. It is purely based on what Rohit and the coach feel is right for the team. There is no agenda, there are no favourites and there is no one who can put his hand on his heart and say he has been hard done by. That's very difficult to achieve, given the vast number of players who have been playing for the country in the last couple of years.'

A Lasting Legacy

Laxman can't stop praising Rohit enough for the fortitude he displayed in the aftermath of the 50-over World Cup disappointment. 'The way he held his poise, it was fabulous,' he gushes. 'The wonderful campaign, the terrible disappointment of the final... To come back from that is very difficult. But to come back in the fashion that Rohit and India did, wow. At the T20 World Cup, India followed the same methodology as the 50-over World Cup, and it takes courage to do that because of what happened in the final in Ahmedabad. In all this, it was Rohit who led the charge from the front.'

The pitches in New York during India's league matches were hardly suitable for club cricket, let alone the T20 World Cup. But once the team moved to the Caribbean for the second phase and the surfaces were a lot more trustworthy, Rohit became the enforcer that he had been seven months ago, in the longer format's showpiece event. 'It was as if he was determined to exact some kind of revenge against Australia for what happened in Ahmedabad,' Laxman says. 'Rohit sensed that India had a great chance to put Australia out of the tournament and he went out and played one of the most brutal knocks I have seen from him. Then, in the semifinal against England, he was again at his attacking best. He led the way in both those games because he knew that he had to lead the way. If he had been timid or circumspect, you never know how many he would have scored and how quickly; you never know what the result would have been if he didn't play in that fashion.

'The others also performed, I am not saying we won those matches only because of Rohit,' he notes. 'But he was the one who set the platform, the way he did throughout the 50-over

The Rise of the Hitman

World Cup. You know, I feel he inspired the team...he just inspired the entire team. The more I think about it, the more I admire his batting, of course, but also his mindset, his attitude, his approach.

'It's perhaps premature to talk a lot about the legacy he will leave behind. But whatever he has done in the last two and a half years, it is enough to show that he is a wonderful leader. Even though the sample size is less compared to the other captains India has had, I feel it's sufficient for him to be hailed as a great leader.'

Anil Kumble takes an equally holistic view, reflecting on Rohit the batter as much as Rohit the captain. 'He's one of the best openers of all time in white-ball cricket,' acknowledges Kumble, 'and his legacy has been the way he's been able to win trophies, both for his franchise and for the country. Yes, the T20 World Cup will certainly be the ultimate feather in his cap. But the way he led in that 50-over World Cup too was amazing. Unfortunately, things didn't work out in the final but that takes nothing away from Rohit.

'And then, just to have the gumption to keep that same attitude in the T20 World Cup despite the loss of a World Cup final just a few months previously, that's not easy to do at all. We saw that against Australia; he smashed them to bits and that to me was the biggest move. He literally took Australia out of the equation; they didn't even make it to the top four (semifinals) and that made a massive difference.

'Rohit reads the game very well; he's very strategic. He knows the pulse of the game very well. All this, plus of course his honesty as batter and captain. People will remember him for his batting and of course he's extremely talented as a player, but there are many other layers to him as well and that will be his legacy. The way he has helped integrate the young players into the national team; every captain goes through that process, right? If you are in the seat for a few years, you always have some players come in and create a niche and they always look up to their first captain. He's only been around for a short period but he has still created that strength of core players—created a template for the next set of players to follow—which is a great thing.'

Vikram Rathour has been involved in various capacities during Rohit's international journey—as selector from 2012 to 2016, the period when he moved up to open the batting in the limited-overs formats, and as the batting coach of the national side from 2019 till the T20 World Cup win in the West Indies in 2024.

'I had the opportunity to observe him as a young player. You just needed to watch him bat, basically, and you knew that he was something special, a special player,' Rathour says. 'But he didn't have a great start to his international career. He played some good innings but also some poor ones. He hadn't sorted out the tempo of his batting. As a selection group, we really backed him because we all believed he was a special player who needed to be groomed and supported as much as possible. And he proved everybody right by then becoming the kind of player he became, right?'

It was after he became the batting coach following the 2019 World Cup semifinal loss that Rathour got to know and work with Rohit closely. 'I started to spend much more

The Rise of the Hitman

time with him, so I got to know him even better. He always had a very sensible mind and a great head on his shoulder. But what stands out with him is that he's a player's captain,' Rathour notes. 'The amount of time he spent with the players was unreal. He would attend every meeting—every batters' meeting, every bowling meeting. If I had a one-on-one session with a batter, he'd be there trying to understand what we were discussing, how it should come out, what is the plan, what are the ideas…

'He spent a lot of time on team strategies—how the team should play, what are the technical changes that are required. He gave a lot of time to the team, which was his great strength. Tactically, he's really, really good. At times, he would make some changes; me and Rahul (Dravid), Paras (Mhambrey, the bowling coach), we'd all be sitting outside and wondering why he had brought on a particular bowler at a particular time. And, more often than not, things would pan out and you'd see that it was the right call, the right thing to do at that time. He keeps surprising you as a captain, which is just great.'

W.V. Raman believes that Rohit will be fondly remembered by history for sparking a sea change in mindset. 'He is the kind of person who believes in the team being put in the forefront, not individuals. That way, the ultimate objectives are the same,' he emphasizes. 'Not that I'm inferring that earlier team management members had different objectives—it's just that it all came together at the right time. Given everything—the size of our country, the unrealistic expectations sometimes of our people—captaining India is not easy.

'Having said that, it was a lot more challenging in the earlier decades but for various reasons—the decision-making from the selectors and the administrators could be very, very whimsical and taken at the drop of a hat. You had a captain who won you the first World Cup out of nowhere being sacked in four months' time. That is the kind of decision-making that used to happen in the decades gone by.

'It's not a question of whether that's right or wrong. But what perhaps is the toughest thing out here now, in today's world, is the phenomenal level of expectations that people have. It's just that they don't think that in a sport a side can lose. They think if a team is involved in a sport, they have to win. That's a given. And especially in cricket, the entire country follows it with such passion. They think India plays, toss is done—that's the only thing that is 50-50. But whatever happens after the toss, at the end of the day they think the scoreboard should show India has won. That's the biggest challenge for the captain now.'

In India especially, everyone and their nephew is a cricket pundit, which means each decision is open to passionate analysis and dissection. 'Any move the captain makes is obviously seen under the lens of a microscope by thousands of people,' Raman says with feeling. 'Those days, you had—at the most—ten journalists travelling with the team and writing on cricket. You were judged objectively by a lesser number of people. Today, it's a question of different views being floated around. You also have these fan-club battles that go on in social media. These are all things that can sometimes get a bit difficult for a captain because, inasmuch as he or she would like to ignore it, somewhere down the line, it comes back to you from

The Rise of the Hitman

people around you. That is the biggest challenge. And from all accounts, it is a challenge Rohit has met quite well.'

Raman is happy that even if it took Rohit leading his side to a World Cup title to firm up his legacy in Indian cricket, he is finally getting his due. 'We live in a country where numbers and results are what people are judged by. It's not the deeds, it's not the efforts that have gone into somebody's tenure as captain or as a player,' he explains. 'It can be a bit unfair at times because it's just sheer numbers; results alone are not the yardstick to judge a person's career or his acumen. Rohit Sharma is obviously now seen differently because of what has happened in the recent past—having that tremendous 50-over campaign in the World Cup which India were unlucky not to win on the day it mattered, and also winning the T20 World Cup.

'But how are we to forget the titles he has won as a franchisee captain? And that is a very, very difficult campaign. The IPL campaign is difficult because there will be tremendous ebbs and flows over a period of eight weeks. Then you play a lot of cricket, there is much travel, there are a lot of things that come into play. And there, he's got to handle a lot of other things as well. It's a multicultural environment; you have players from different countries. If somebody can manage all that, somebody can get the best out of those guys time after time, obviously there is something to him (as a) captain. To win as many as five IPL titles, that's great. That needs to be appreciated as well.'

Raman feels that, in some ways, Rohit is a victim of the expectations he has triggered and the benchmarks he has set. 'What happens is that sometimes, we tend to take things for granted. We think, "Oh, Rohit Sharma, he's going to win everything." The sights we set for a guy are a bit difficult for him to live up to all the time. Is it a backhanded compliment that you expect him to win as captain all the time? Yes, that's what we think. Because he's won five IPLs, we think, "Rohit Sharma, leader of Mumbai Indians, he's handled the side well, he's won five times. Who's the other guy who's done that? Another guy who's done that, who has won ICC titles? (M.S.) Dhoni." So, you think Rohit is going to do the same thing for the country, no big deal.

'Because he's been around for a long time, because he's a very good performer, the expectations are a bit too high. But isn't it one of those great stories? Again, I go back five years in time. You would never have thought in, let's say, October 2019, that Rohit Sharma would lead the Indian Test team because you didn't even know if he was going to survive in Test cricket. But look at how far he has come on as player and leader, look at the heights he has taken the team to. I will remember Rohit fondly for that—for his resilience, for his mental strength, for his ability to reinvent himself as batter and leader—as much as for the trophies he has stacked up in his cabinet.'

Rohit is at that stage of his cricketing life where long-term goals and ambitions might not be his prime focus. Will he be around at the next 50-over World Cup in 2027? Unlikely. Will he spearhead India's title defence at the home T20 World Cup in 2026? Most certainly not, given that he has retired internationally from the 20-over format. Sports can be fickle and cricket even more so. Therefore, to hazard what the future holds can be a perilous and foolhardy exercise.

But tomorrow can wait.

It's the here and now that Rohit is firmly entrenched in, not very interested in wondering how history will remember him, determined to drive the team forward, to espouse the motto of inclusivity and togetherness, and to always remind his mates—if they need reminding—that there is nothing greater than the power of the collective.

Epilogue

Transposing the results from one format to another is one of the more common pastimes among cricket followers. India had had a poor run in Test cricket between October and January, losing six and winning just one of eight matches. So the perception was that Rohit Sharma—more than his team—was under pressure heading into the 50-over ICC Champions Trophy, revived by the world body after eight years.

The build-up to the tournament was fraught with obstacles. The Indian government refused permission for its cricket team to travel to Pakistan; in 2021, the Pakistan Cricket Board had been conferred with the privilege of hosting the tournament, marking the return of global cricket to that country for the first time since 1996 and the 50-over World Cup which it co-hosted alongside India and Sri Lanka, in happier times. Once it was clear that there was no chance of India playing in Pakistan, the International Cricket Council scrambled to find an acceptable compromise. The PCB was understandably miffed that while its team played in India during the 2011 50-over World Cup, the 2016 T20 Word Cup and the 2023 50-over World Cup, India continued to refuse to travel across the border. It was keen to extract its pound of flesh.

Therefore, while agreeing to a hybrid model where India would play all their matches in Dubai while the rest of the tournament would proceed in Rawalpindi, Karachi and Lahore, the PCB secured a guarantee from the ICC that in all future global events where India would be hosts—be it at the senior or junior levels, in the 50-over or T20 formats, for men or for women—Pakistan too would play their matches at a neutral venue.

Under the hybrid arrangement for this Champions Trophy in February-March 2025, Pakistan themselves would hop across to Dubai to play India in their Group A league fixture. Dubai and the Emirates Cricket Board were guaranteed four matches—all three of India's group outings, as well as the first semifinal on 4 March, irrespective of whether India reached that stage or not. Should India make the 9 March final, that too would be hosted in Dubai. If India failed to qualify, the final would be held on the same date in Lahore.

This schedule was officially announced on 24 December 2024 and met with casual indifference worldwide. Everyone accepted that under the circumstances, it was the best possible solution and the only available compromise. That narrative would change as the tournament progressed, as Rohit and his side notched up one convincing win after another. Suddenly, there was talk of the tournament being 'designed' to facilitate an Indian triumph, of the 'unfair advantage' Rohit's men enjoyed because they played all their matches in Dubai, and therefore would have a firsthand taste of the conditions and be better placed than the others to further their campaign.

Did India enjoy an 'unfair advantage'? Potentially yes.

Epilogue

Not so much because they would have knowledge and experience of how the pitches at the Dubai International Stadium behaved—everyone knows the character of the soil and the nature of the tracks and anyone who claims otherwise clearly has been lax when it comes to homework—but because they could stay in the same hotel for 25 days (if they reached the final); because they didn't have to pack their bags every three days and fly from one city to another; because they were spared bleary eyes stemming from late-night finishes and early morning flights.

The gradually building whispers snowballed into a crescendo once India swatted Australia aside and sealed their place in the final. Remarkably, while everyone who had an opinion railed at the unfairness of it all, the team that earned the right to challenge India in the final, New Zealand, showed the greatest equanimity, refraining from singing from the same hymn sheet as the rest. Perhaps because they weren't looking to justify a possible early exit, they focused on themselves rather than on the developments beyond their control. The loudest carpers—the English of course—didn't even threaten a flight to Dubai except to transit to London, losing all their Group B matches. In the middle of their miserable run, Jos Buttler stepped down as the ODI captain.

India were totally unaffected by whatever was being said and written around them. During their time in Dubai, they were purposeful in their training sessions, managing the long gaps and short turnaround time between matches (twice) with common sense and aplomb. They had reached Dubai five days before their opening game against Bangladesh on 20 February and used that time judiciously, re-familiarizing themselves with their new 'home' for the next three and a half weeks, where they had a glorious chance to rewrite history.

In the year and a half leading up to the Champions Trophy, Jasprit Bumrah had been his team's most influential figure. He was stunning during the home World Cup in 2023, the Player of the Tournament when Rohit lifted the T20 World Cup in the Americas in June 2024, and the Player of the Series despite India's 1-3 loss in the Test series in Australia which ended in January 2025. Bumrah hadn't recovered fully from the lower back injury that prevented him from bowling in the second innings of the final Test in Sydney and was therefore left out of the final Champions Trophy squad after having figured in the initial provisional list of 15. His place was taken by Harshit Rana, who boasted only three Internationals, all against England in February 2025.

How would India cope without Bumrah? Especially given how undercooked the Indian bowling attack was? Mohammed Shami was a seasoned campaigner but had played only a handful of matches from November 2024 after injuring his Achilles' heel during the 2023 World Cup. Kuldeep Yadav, the left-arm wrist-spinner, was just coming off surgery to fix a sports hernia problem. Arshdeep Singh, the third specialist pacer behind Shami and Rana, had played a mere nine ODIs. Without Bumrah, India looked lighter on the bowling front than ever before.

Just before the deadline for the announcement of the final

squad passed, India made an interesting but eventually decisive change to their 15. Rohit has been a great believer in playing the conditions, which is why he had packed the T20 World Cup party with four spinners. For Dubai, he wanted a fifth tweaker.

Five spinners in a team of 15? Making up the third of the entire squad?

Madness, right?

No, no... Not madness. The late addition was Varun Chakravarthy, the leg-spin-cum-googly bowler who had found a second wind in international cricket. The 33-year-old Chakravarthy had taken 14 wickets in five T20Is against England in January-February 2025, and Rohit was convinced the man with a degree in architecture would orchestrate India's challenge in Dubai, on worn-out surfaces late in the season. That conviction manifested itself in Chakravarthy winning the Player of the Match award on his Champions Trophy debut against New Zealand in the group fixture and translated to nine wickets in three outings, one of several driving forces behind India's unchecked march to the title.

∞

Of the five spinners in the squad, three were proper all-rounders—Ravindra Jadeja, Axar Patel and Washington Sundar (who, like Arshdeep and Rishabh Pant, didn't play a single game). Hardik Pandya provided the seam-up all-rounder option, K.L. Rahul slotted in as the wicketkeeper-batter at number six so that the left-handed Axar could split a right-heavy batting order by coming out at number five. Shubman Gill, Rohit's deputy,

The Rise of the Hitman

came into the tournament ranked the No. 1 ODI batter in the world and took up the number two position in the order; Shreyas Iyer at number four was pivotal with his multi-gear propensity. That left two of the greatest white-ball batters of all time to plug the first and third spots.

Rohit had had a forgettable run in Test cricket but warmed up for the tournament with his thirty-second ODI century against England in Cuttack, on 9 February 2025. The outside world might have thought he had bought himself breathing space, but Rohit has never entertained such thinking. He knew what he had to do on the slow tracks in Dubai, where Powerplay runs would be worth their weight in gold. He also knew that Virat Kohli, the maker of the most ODI hundreds, was a big-stage player who would be energized by the occasion.

The skipper and his predecessor made telling impacts. Rohit's cameos were vital without being decisive in the games before the final, while Kohli fished out his chasing garb, shepherding challenging run-chases against Pakistan and Australia (in the semis) with efforts of 100 not out and 84, respectively. While the two senior statesmen were doing their thing, India extracted crucial contributions from everyone who played—every single of the combined 12 players fielded in five games. If ever there was team effort, it was this.

Gill made a hundred in the opening victory against Bangladesh, the same game where Shami responded to Bumrah's absence with a five-wicket haul. Iyer was consistently outstanding, reading situations perfectly and batting accordingly. Rohit called him the 'unsung hero', which he probably was. But he was a hero nevertheless. Axar was sensible at number five, chipping in with small but pivotal hands, while Rahul was sensational at number six, taking to his new role with practised ease. And it was indeed practised—at the ICC Academy ground where India had their training sessions, he perfected range-hitting against soft balls, aware he would often be required to tee off from ball one. Once he was put in those positions in matches—against Bangladesh, Australia in the semifinal and New Zealand in the final—he fed off recent muscle memory to remain unbeaten during each of those successful chases.

Pandya was electric, rounding off the top seven with panache and swagger. Such was India's batting consistency that Jadeja, who averages 32.62 and has a strike-rate of 85.44 in 204 ODIs, was barely pressed into service. He did leave his mark though, with the boundary that allowed Rohit to wrap his hands around the title.

The captain might not have had the most fulfilling tournament numerically, but except in the two games against New Zealand, he scored at well over a run a ball. His 36-ball 41 in the opener against Bangladesh set the tone during what should have been—but wasn't—a regulation chase of 228. And even though he lost all five tosses, it made no impact on him or his boys that they had to react to what was in front of them instead of being in a position to do all the running.

Rohit saved his best for last, with a magnificent 76 that set up the four-wicket triumph in the final. He blazed a splendid trail in the first ten overs, destroying the bowling with typically bruising stroke-play, then bedding in against an ageing ball to construct an innings that ended with a rare rush of blood dictated by the scoreboard coming to a standstill. The value of

The Rise of the Hitman

his knock was recognized by the adjudicators who bestowed on him the honour of being the Player of the Final. What a fitting way to end a campaign that he masterminded with such calmness and intelligence for five matches in a row.

One of the great challenges of having four very good spinners—two of them wristies capable of altering outcomes in an over or two—is knowing when and how to use them. From game three onwards—Rana played the first two before making way for Chakravarthy—India fielded Kuldeep, Axar, Jadeja and Chakravarthy. The league outing against the Kiwis was the first time in their ODI history that India had included four specialist spinners in their playing XI, and the wisdom of that move was immediately apparent when Chakravarthy walked away with five wickets.

Rohit handled this quartet adroitly. Jadeja apart, the other three bowled inside the first ten overs more than once. He used the two wrist-spinners in wicket-taking capacities, relying on the left-arm finger spin of Axar and Jadeja to control the scoring and go through their overs quickly during the middle stages of an innings. The foursome operated superbly in tandem, helped by their captain's faith in them and in the role-clarity provided by the leadership group of Rohit and Gautam Gambhir. India often bowled in the best batting conditions and batted in the most favourable bowling conditions and yet ended up winning two games by six wickets, two others (including the final) by four wickets, and the only match in which they batted first by 44 runs. If that doesn't present the picture of a dominant, unstoppable force, nothing else will.

India celebrated with gusto, as is to be expected. After

Epilogue

all, they had become the first side to lift the Champions Trophy thrice. It was their second triumph in three editions—split by a loss to Pakistan in the 2017 final at The Oval—and their second ICC title in less than eight months. Rohit had joined Mahendra Singh Dhoni as the only Indian captains with more than one ICC title to their name. The circumstances under which this trophy was secured must have made the campaign even sweeter, even more memorable.

Throughout the tournament, there was talk of this being Rohit's final international dance, no matter the outcome. Several thundered that he would retire whenever India's campaign ended, as if they knew more than the protagonist himself. After fielding all questions at the end-of-the-final press conference, the trophy sitting proudly by his side, Rohit said with an enigmatic smile, 'One more thing. I'm not going to retire from this format; just to make sure that no rumours are spread moving forward.'

Enough said, Rohit Sharma.

Enough said.

Acknowledgements

They say it takes a village to write a book. All right, they don't say it, but it *does* take a village to write a book.

An overwhelming majority of the people I reached out to during the writing of this book were readily forthcoming with their views, making time to oblige my sometimes-unreasonable demands. To all of them, I will remain perennially grateful.

Huge thanks to:

Rohit Sharma for being the man and player he is, and Ritika for penning the most lovely foreword;

Kapish and Rudra at Rupa for entrusting me with the responsibility of reliving Rohit's glorious cricketing journey, and Shakya for his commitment to editing;

Cricketing giants Rahul Dravid, Anil Kumble, V.V.S. Laxman, W.V. Raman, Yuvraj Singh and Dinesh Karthik for their time and wisdom;

R. Sridhar, Vikram Rathour, Ajit Agarkar, Parthiv Patel, Abhishek Nayar, Mayank Agarwal, Dhawal Kulkarni, and Dinesh Lad and Basu Shanker—several of them old friends and great storytellers, and all of whom have been closely associated with Rohit;

Manuja Veerappa and Vishaal Loganathan, my twin pillars of strength and support;

V. Balaji, Madhu Jawali, K.C.Vijaya Kumar and G.Viswanath, my other go-to people for inputs and (sometimes) sanity;

Surjeet Yadav for the wonderful cover photograph and for all the other evocative images;

A host of colleagues and friends (many of them both), including Satish Viswanathan, Clayton Murzello, G. Krishnan, Vijay Lokapally, Rex Clementine, S. Balasubramaniam, Rathan Kumar, Anand Subramaniam and Moulin Parikh (the last two from the BCCI's media team);

My father, for keeping me on my toes, constantly monitoring the progress of the book and repeatedly reminding me of the deadlines;

All other friends who helped me along the way with words of encouragement and nuggets of information.

Index

2007 50-over World Cup, 147
2007 T20 World Cup, 17, 125
2011 50-over World Cup, 71, 183
2011 World Cup, 167
2022 T20 Asia Cup, 124
2023 Campaign, 130
2023 World Cup, 38, 137, 141, 166, 186
2024 T20 World Cup, 151

Afridi, Shahid, 25, 60
Agarkar, Ajit, xix, 7, 56, 94, 106, 107, 119, 124, 125, 193
Anderson, James, 104, 105, 106
Arun, B., 45, 144
Ashwin, R., 86, 100, 157
Asia Cup, 7, 38, 124, 129, 159, 160

Azharuddin, Mohammad, xv, 87, 121

Badrinath, S., 27
Bandra, 26, 34, 35, 162, 168
Bangar, Sanjay, 90, 144
Bird, Jackson, 10
Board of Control for Cricket in India (BCCI), 6, 14, 24, 118, 144, 173, 194
Borivali, xi, 2, 3, 6, 8, 23, 162, 166, 168
Bracken, Nathan, 22
Bresnan, Tim, 40
Bridgetown, xi, xxi, 140, 141, 155
Broad, Stuart, 18, 106
Bumrah, Jasprit, xx, xxi, xxiii, xxvi, xxvii, 78, 100, 116, 118, 131, 140, 155, 186, 188

Buttler, Jos, xxiv, 140, 185

Chahal, Yuzvendra, 78
Chakravarthy, Varun, 187, 190
Challenger Series, 13, 146
Champions Trophy, 40, 183, 184, 186, 187, 190
Chappell, Greg, 13
Chawla, Piyush, 9, 11
Chennai Super Kings, 57, 63, 68, 138
Civil Service Cricket Club, 15
Clarke, Michael, 22
Cooch Behar Trophy, 10
Cummins, Pat, 80, 134

Dalmiya, Jagmohan, 76
Dar, Aleem, 75
de Kock, Quinton, xxv
Deccan Chargers, 23, 25, 31, 58, 59, 61, 62, 68, 159
Delhi Daredevils, 57, 64
Deodhar Trophy, 11, 12
Dernbach, Jade, 40
detached attachment, 83, 173
Dev, Kapil, xvii, xxvii, 36, 118
Dhawan, Shikhar, 11, 40, 41, 42, 72, 80, 122
Dhiman, Gaurav, 10
Dhoni, M.S., xiii, xv, xvii, xviii, xix, 13, 17, 18, 19, 24, 25, 28, 29, 38, 39, 47, 48, 57, 63, 68, 69, 82, 83, 86, 113, 116, 118, 122, 161, 181, 191
Dilip, T., 132
Dombivli, 2
double hundred, 42, 49, 50, 152
Dravid, Rahul, xii, xix, xx, 13, 15, 17, 25, 27, 28, 29, 57, 87, 95, 118, 124, 144, 145, 146, 147, 148, 149, 150, 151, 152, 153, 154, 155, 156, 157, 159, 173, 178, 193
du Plessis, Faf, 78
Dubai T20 World Cup, 11
Dube, Shivam, xxii, 169

Eden Gardens, 13, 45, 51, 64
Emirates Cricket Board, 184

Finch, Aaron, 72
Finn, Steven, 40
Fletcher, Duncan, xiii, 38
Flintoff, Andrew, 165
Franklin, James, 62
full-time captain, 117

Gambhir, Gautam, 11, 15, 19, 21, 38, 39, 40, 48, 165, 190
Ganguly, Sourav, 15, 17, 41, 57,

Index

58, 87, 110, 118, 144
Gibbs, Herschelle, 25, 60
Gilchrist, Adam, 25, 41, 60, 61
Giles Shield, 5
Gill, Shubman, 130, 132, 187, 188
Gould, Ian, 75
Greenidge, Gordon, 41

Hall, Andrew, 15
Hansen, John, 21
Haque, Mominul, 105
Harris Shield, 5
Hayden, Matthew, 41
Haynes, Desmond, 41
Head, Travis, 135
Hendricks, Reeza, xxv
Hitman, 47, 55, 158
Hogg, Brad, 22
Hope, James, 22
Hossain, Rubel, 75, 115
Hossain, Shahadat, 27

ICC title, 181, 191
ICC tournament, 41, 122, 148, 149, 154
impact knocks, 110
Indian cricket, 40, 62, 66, 89, 92, 118, 120, 123, 144, 150, 151, 169, 172, 174, 180

Indian Premier League, xix, 1, 24, 57
India Under-19, xii, 10, 144
International Cricket Council (ICC), 33, 75, 76, 154, 183, 184, 189
IPL, xv, xix, xxii, xxiv, 1, 23, 24, 26, 31, 37, 57, 59, 60, 61, 62, 63, 65, 67, 68, 69, 70, 99, 113, 119, 125, 138, 143, 149, 155, 159, 180
Iyer, Shreyas, 128, 129, 132, 188

Jadeja, Ravindra, xx, xxiii, xxiv, 11, 83, 100, 131, 138, 140, 157, 187, 189, 190
Jamieson, Kyle, 101
Jansen, Marco, xxvii
Jayasuriya, Sanath, 62
Jayawardene, Mahela, 105
Johnson, Mitchell, 22, 65

Kallis, Jacques, 15, 28
Kalpesh Koli tournament, 6
Kamal, Mustafa, 75, 76
Karthik, Dinesh, 15, 28, 63, 83, 115, 137, 161, 193
Kemp, Justin, 18
Kensington Oval, xxi, xxvii, xxviii

Khan, Sohail, 73
Kings XI Punjab, 57
Kirsten, Gary, 25
Klaasen, Heinrich, xxiv, xxv, xxvi
Kohli, Virat, xiii, xiv, xx, xxii, xxv, xxvii, xxviii, 31, 38, 40, 42, 50, 54, 73, 77, 79, 80, 85, 86, 87, 89, 90, 99, 100, 113, 114, 116, 117, 118, 119, 122, 123, 124, 130, 132, 140, 143, 144, 145, 146, 157, 170, 173, 188
Kolkata Knight Riders, 57, 64
KSCA MRF Trophy, 9, 58
Kulkarni, Dhawal, 167, 193
Kumble, Anil, 63, 64, 65, 68, 88, 95, 96, 126, 144, 176, 193

Labuschagne, Marnus, 135
Lad, Dinesh, xv, 3, 4, 5, 6, 7, 14, 17, 26, 33, 34, 54, 193
Lahiri, Saurasish, 13
Lamb, Allan, 105
Laxman, V.V.S., 27, 28, 29, 30, 44, 48, 49, 50, 53, 54, 58, 59, 60, 61, 66, 79, 87, 107, 108, 109, 111, 124, 127, 159, 173, 174, 175, 193

Lee, Brett, 22, 59
Lord's, 36, 104

M. Chinnaswamy Stadium, 9, 43
Maharaj, Keshav, xxv
Malinga, Lasith, 62, 65
man-management, xiv, 123, 124
Markram, Aiden, xxv
Mendis, Ajantha, 32
Mhambrey, Paras, 178
Miller, David, xxv, xxvi, xxvii, xxviii
Mishra, Amit, 12
Modi, Lalit, 24
Mongia, Dinesh, 12
Monkeygate, 21
Morkel, Morne, 18, 28
Morris, Chris, 78
Mumbai Indians, xiv, xix, xxvi, 57, 60, 61, 62, 63, 64, 66, 67, 68, 69, 99, 113, 119, 138, 143, 169, 181
Mushtaq Ali Trophy, 13

Nabi, Abid, 12
Nadeem, Shahbaz, 9
Narendra Modi Stadium, xviii, 128, 135
Nassau Country International

Cricket Stadium, xx
Nayar, Abhishek, 34, 71, 137, 160, 193
Nidahas Trophy, 114, 143
NKP Salve Trophy, 13
Nortje, Anrich, xxv
Ntini, Makhaya, 18

O'Brien, Niall, 15
ODI century, 51, 188
ODI hundred, 42, 77, 188
Old Trafford, 81

Pakistan Cricket Board, 183
Pandey, Manish, 115
Pandya, Hardik, xviii, 79, 124, 131, 187
Pant, Rishabh, xxvii, 100, 105, 187
Parnell, Wayne, 28
Patel, Axar, xviii, xxii, xxiii, xxiv, xxvi, 187, 188, 190
Patel, Parthiv, 11, 12, 67, 68, 69, 70, 169, 170, 193
Patel, Samit, 40
Pathan, Yusuf, 33
PCA Stadium, 40
PCB, 183, 184
Permaul, Veerasammy, 87
Philander, Vernon, 18, 92

Player of the Final, 190
Player of the Match, 18, 187
Player of the Series, 186
playing XI, 66, 67, 73, 124, 140, 190
Pollard, Kieron, 62
Pollock, Shaun, 18
Ponting, Ricky, xiv, 21, 22, 63, 64
Pope, Ollie, 138, 157
Prasad, Venkatesh, 17, 58
Procter, Mike, 21
Pujara, Cheteshwar, 10, 87, 105

Queen's Sports Club, 31

Rabada, Kagiso, xxv, xxviii, 78, 92
Rahane, Ajinkya, 7, 38, 39, 99, 118, 147
Rahman, Mustafizur, 116
Rahul, K.L., 55, 81, 89, 103, 128, 157, 187
Rajasthan Royals, 57
Rajput, Lalchand, 17
Raman, W.V., 43, 52, 53, 54, 74, 93, 94, 110, 111, 121, 122, 178, 179, 180, 193
Rana, Harshit, 186
Ranji Trophy, ix, 13, 26, 29, 125

Rathour, Vikram, 45, 71, 90, 102, 141, 144, 177, 193
red-ball opener, xiii, 89, 110, 111
Richardson, Dave, 75
Richards, Viv, xxviii
Rising Pune Supergiant, 69
Robinson, Ollie, 104
Root, Joe, 40, 104
Rose Bowl, 78
Royal Challengers Bangalore, 57, 63

Saha, Wriddhiman, 27
Sajdeh, Ritika, 148, 150, 163, 166, 170, 193
Samaira, 98, 150, 165
Sangakkara, Kumar, 82
Sehwag, Virendra, 17, 38, 43, 48, 57
Shamsi, Tabraiz, xxv, 78
Shankar, Vijay, 115
Shanker, Basu, 84, 193
Sharma, Joginder, 12
Shastri, Ravi, xiii, 14, 45, 88, 89, 90, 93, 111, 118, 144
Sheikh Zayed Stadium, 12
Shukla, Ravikant, xii
Singh, Arshdeep, xxiii, xxvii, 156, 186, 187

Singh, Gagandeep, 12
Singh, Harbhajan, 17, 21, 62, 170
Singh, Rinku, xxii
Singh, Robin, 17
Singh, Yuvraj, 13, 15, 17, 18, 19, 20, 21, 28, 29, 33, 35, 57, 118, 165, 166, 169, 193
Smith, Steve, 69
Sodhi, Reetinder Singh, 12
Solanki, Vikram, 18
Sridhar, R., 40, 80, 101, 144, 193
Steyn, Dale, 28
Stubbs, Tristan, xxv
Sundar, Washington, 69, 115, 187
Symonds, Andrew, 21, 25

T20 century, 63
T20 World Cup, 2024, 138
Tahir, Imran, 78
Tendulkar, Sachin, xiii, 1, 15, 17, 21, 22, 31, 35, 38, 41, 42, 43, 46, 48, 49, 57, 58, 62, 63, 85, 86, 87, 93, 95, 121
Test hundred, 102, 105, 112
Thaker, Bhavik, 11
Thakur, Shardul, 105, 131

Index

The Oval, 78, 80, 104, 191
Tiwary, Manoj, 14, 29
Top End Series, 13
touch player, 52
Tredwell, James, 40
tri-series, 20, 21, 23, 26, 27, 38, 49, 59, 73

Under-14, 5
Under-16, 5, 6, 14
Under-17, 6, 7, 8, 14
Under-17 Asia Cup, 9
Under-19, xii, 10, 59, 144
Under-19 World Cup, 10
Uthappa, Robin, 17, 21

Vengsarkar, Dilip, 7
Vihari, Hanuma, 100

Vijay Hazare Trophy, 10, 13
Vijay Merchant Trophy, 7, 9
Vinoo Mankad Trophy, 10
Vishwaroopam, 41

WACA ground, 21
white-ball opener, 36
Woakes, Chris, 104
World Cup-winning captain, xxix
World Test Championship, 88, 100, 127, 155
Wright, John, 63

Yadav, Kuldeep, xxiii, xxvi, 124, 131, 140, 186, 190
Yadav, Suryakumar, xxiii, xxvii, xxviii, 131, 140, 169